The Rise and Fall of the United States

The Rise and Fall of the United States

Harold J. Farrall

VANTAGE PRESS
New York

FIRST EDITION

Published by Vantage Press, Inc.
516 West 34th Street, New York, New York 10001

Manufactured in the United States of America
ISBN: 0-533-10224-3

Library of Congress Catalog Card No.: 92-93307

0 9 8 7 6 5 4 3 2 1

To my mother, Olive Almira (Frazell) Farrall, who from my point of view was the greatest person to live in the twentieth century. Through hardships and misfortunes and with Bible guidance she raised eight good, Christian children who were outstanding citizens. During all the time while I was growing up at home, I do not even remember hearing a swear word or a discouraging word in our home. Mother followed the commandments and tenets of the Bible, and probably her favorite was the "golden rule" (Matthew 7:12).

Contents

Preface

I have often wondered why the United States came into being and why it became the greatest nation on earth. Also, over the years I have wondered about why other things happened around the world and why other events that affected me personally occurred. I turned to the Bible to try to find the answers to these things. I discovered that the answers to most problems and most questions are in the Bible. One just has to search for them. I found in the Bible the answer to why the United States was formed and also what is going to happen to the United States. It is very exciting to discover who we are and why we are. There is no true knowledge except that knowledge that is revealed from God. How is knowledge revealed? The Bible says to search the Scriptures daily with all readiness of mind like the Bereans did and knowledge will be revealed to you (Acts 17:10–12; Isaiah 28:9–13). It takes many months of study for knowledge to be revealed to a person (Proverbs 28:5).

People don't seem to realize that the commandments and tenets in the Old Testament of the Bible apply for all time, not just for those olden times. Jesus did away with the animal sacrifices, rituals, and circumcision, but the commandments and tenets of the Bible were retained. The commandments and tenets of the Bible apply to our modern times now (Deuteronomy 21:18–21). Anyone who wants to be a Christian and be saved must follow the commandments and tenets of the Bible.

A thousand years is only one day for God (II Peter 3:8). So all the history of our civilization as we know it was only a six-day period for God. The seventh day is reserved for the period of time when Jesus returns to earth and establishes his world government.

The people of the United States have forgotten, or perhaps they never knew, how and why the United States was formed and grew into the greatest single nation on the face of the earth. (Great Britain was greater at one time, but they were a group of nations rather than a single nation.) The answer is in the Bible (Genesis 48).

I realized that there needed to be a book, in brief form, which could be read and understood in one sitting, recording why the United States became a great nation and why the United States will go into decline and captivity. All this is written out in the Bible and can be understood once God reveals to you knowledge that is in the Bible. This book pertains to the United States, but the prophecies also pertain to Great Britain, because the inheritance given by God to Abraham, then to Isaac, then to Jacob (changed to Israel) was passed on to Ephraim and Manasseh through Joseph, their father. Ephraim is Great Britain and Manasseh is the United States (Genesis 48).

Everything that was and everything that is comes from God (Genesis 1; Nehemiah 9:6; Job 12:23; Colossians 1:15–17). God created the heavens and earth in six days (Exodus 20:11). Humans were given 6,000 years to develop the 144,000 elect required to rule the earth with Jesus Christ and to develop a Christian civilization (II Peter 3:8). Humans will fail to develop a Christian civilization because Satan controls the affairs of the earth now (Revelation 12:7–9; I Peter 5:8; Job 2:2). At the end of the 6,000 years God's son, Jesus Christ, will return to the earth a second time to take over the rule of the earth and destroy all nations and peoples that do not conform to the commandments and principles of the Bible (II Thessalonians 2:2). Then it will take 1,000 years to sort out those who will conform and be saved for eternal life (Revelation 20:1–4). After the 7,000 (6,000 plus 1,000) years, there will be a resurrection of those who have died for judgment as to whether they will have eternal life or be destroyed (Revelation 20:4–15). God's word is recorded in the Bible by his prophets and his disciples. Gog and Magog, who will try to destroy Jesus Christ and his new world order, are the peoples of Russia, Asia, and its islands and Libya and Ethiopia, except the nation that calls itself Israel now (Revelation 20:7–8; Ezekiel 38:1–6).

There have been many attempts by various people to determine just how long human life has been on this earth, from Adam to this date. Now, with the modern computers and the information in the Bible concerning generations of people and ages of people, the date of Adam's creation should be determined pretty close. I have heard of one estimation that Adam could have been created about 4004 B.C. Others have claimed that the 6,000-year period is nearly over. That doesn't leave much time for civilization as we know it.

During the 6,000-year period there have always been a very small number of individuals, since Noah, who have followed the principles of the Bible and thus kept God's church alive. When Jesus returns to earth (Revelation 19), the 144,000 who have followed the principles of the Bible and are qualified to rule the earth with him will be resurrected or, if still living, will be changed in the twinkling of an eye from mortal to immortal (I Corinthians 15:51–53). These people will be saved to rule the world with Jesus Christ. It will be a dictatorship (Revelation 20:4–6).

The 144,000 (Revelation 14:1–5) will come from the twelve tribes of Israel. There will be 12,000 from each tribe (Revelation 7:4–8). The tribe of Joseph is split into two tribes, namely Ephraim and Manasseh. Ephraim is called Joseph in Revelation 7:8. The tribe of Dan is not included because, I believe, of their warlike and terrorist activities. Thus, because Dan is excluded, there are still only twelve tribes rather than thirteen.

The twelve tribes of Israel are the descendants of Jacob that were taken into captivity by the Assyrians and Babylonians (I Kings and II Kings). Ten tribes were taken over to the Caspian Sea area where the Caucasian Mountains are located. These are the tribes of Ephraim, Manasseh, Dan, Reuben, Zebulon, Issachar, Asher, Naphtali, Gad, and Simeon. They later migrated west and north from there into Europe, the British Isles, the United States, Canada, Australia, and South Africa. In the case of the tribes of Judah, Benjamin, and Levi, they were taken captive later by Babylon and then later scattered into all the nations of the world. The people of Israel were forbidden by God to take strange wives, that is, those that were not of the tribes of Israel (Ezra 10:2–3, 10–19; Nehemiah 13:3, 23–27; Genesis 24:1–4). So the tribes of Israel to this day are the white peoples who migrated to the west and north from the area of the Caucasian Mountains and who scattered to all nations of the world from Jerusalem. The ten tribes who migrated from the Caucasian Mountain area are even as of this date referred to as Caucasian.

The people of Israel are God's chosen people forever (II Samuel 7:24). The throne of Israel, which was David's throne, and the house of David are established forever (I Chronicles 22:5–10). There is evidence that this throne is now located in England, which is Ephraim, son of Joseph, and has been there for a long time (Genesis 49:22–26).

The throne (stone) of Israel is that on which the kings of England sit when they are crowned, according to historians. Some say that Jeremiah took it with him when he escaped from the Babylonians and journeyed to Ireland. Israel is God's right hand to control the major activities on the earth and to destroy evil nations (Jeremiah 51:19–23). That is why God inspired and permitted Israel to build great navies, great armies, and great air forces in order to be able to destroy the despots of the world. That is why God permitted Israel to build the atomic weapons. The people of Israel are the fair people (white people) who were originally captives in Egypt and whom God rescued from Egypt (Leviticus 26:12–13). God then gave them the choicest lands of the world that had been inhabited by heathen (Psalms 105:42–44).

The entire Bible was written to and for the Israelites and those strangers who want to become saved (Ephesians 3:3–5). God got his word to his chosen people through angels of the Lord and also prophets, by means of dreams. The prophets then recorded the dreams along with actual events that occurred, and thus we have the Bible (Numbers 12:6). On occasion God spoke to an individual, such as Adam and Moses. His voice is like thunder (Job 37:4–5) or like a trumpet (Revelation 1:10).

This book is not to put anyone, any tribe, or any nation down, but its only purpose is to explain why people and tribes are destined to play their part on the earth's stage for this 6,000-year period and to reveal at the end-time knowledge that has been closed up and thus not understood until the end-time. (Daniel 12:9). This book is not intended to get anyone to change his life-style or to convert anyone to Christianity. The Bible says each person is to choose (Joshua 24:15) which way he will go (Deuteronomy 30:19–20).

This book is to show why world events occurred as they did. God controls what goes on around the earth to a certain extent, and there is no way that anyone or any tribe can win against God in any dispute that they may have concerning their role in the affairs of life. Anyone, no matter who or from what tribe, can become a member of God's Kingdom. You have to accept Jesus Christ as your savior and follow the commandments (the Ten Commandments) without deviation. Anyone who breaks even one of the commandments is in serious trouble with God (Exodus 20; Matthew 5:19, 19:17; John 8:51, 14:15, 15:10).

It is interesting and revealing that most of the great inventions in the world have been made by Israelites. God stirs up *his* people and puts ideas into their minds. That is why inventions are made, why new lands are discovered and developed, and why wars are won. God inspires his people to do those things. That is why a heathen nation could never outdo an Israelite nation unless through trickery, thievery, or bribery they steal innovations already developed and the Israelite nation has become so evil that God turned his back on them.

Israel is God's servant and any who strive against Israel will die (Isaiah 41:8–12). Israel is commanded to give instruction to the Gentiles (Isaiah 42:1–6, 49:6). Gentiles are those peoples who are not Israelites, who are not Jews, but have a form of religion acknowledging a savior but rejecting his message and observing rituals rather than the commandments of God (I Thessalonians 4:5). The heathen are those who worship strange gods or no gods or are atheists (Psalms 135:15; Matthew 18:17). The Lord God is the only God (I Kings 8:60).

The rituals and ordinances of Old Testament times, such as animal sacrifices, were abolished by Jesus (Colossians 2:14). Also, circumcision was abolished (Galatians

5:2–6; I Corinthians 7:18–19). The Ten Commandments were retained and in fact strengthened by adding to love the commandments and one's neighbor (Matthew 22:36–40; Mark 12:28–31; John 14:15, 15:10).

In the latter days of our civilization, knowledge will be revealed to the Saints (Colossians 1:25–26; Revelation 1:19). The God of the Bible is the only God (Isaiah 44:6–11, 45:5–7). God created the heavens, the earth, and man (Isaiah 45:12; Genesis 1; Revelation 4:11). This proves that those who think that man evolved know very little of what is in the Bible.

The Saints are God's elect, the 144,000, who will be rescued and who will be protected from the great tribulation (Revelation 7). Many other Israelites will survive the tribulation, even though they will suffer and be in captivity for a short time prior to the tribulation. Also, many other people will survive the tribulation (Revelation 7:14–17).

Satan rules the earth now, but only with God's permission (Job 1:6–12, 2:2; I Peter 5:8). At the end-time of our civilization, God will chain Satan up so he cannot rule the earth (Revelation 20:1–3). Because Satan is in control now is the reason why there is so much evil in the world today and why there can be no peace and why there is so much destruction and killing. Satan is not permitted to kill God's elect—the 144,000 (Job 1:6–12; I Chronicles 16:22).

At the time of Noah all the inhabitants of the earth were destroyed except for Noah and his family. There were eight people in Noah's family (I Peter 3:20), which consisted of Noah, his wife, and their three sons and their wives. This destruction was because all the inhabitants of the earth, except Noah, had become so evil that God did not want them around anymore. So all the people living today are descendants of Noah. Gods likes variety. You see it in the flowers, the birds, the mammals, etc. The sons of Noah were Shem, Ham, and Japheth. The descendants of Shem are the white people. These people originally settled in the areas of modern-day Iraq, Syria, and the Arabian Peninsula. The descendants of Ham are the black people. These people were originally settled in modern-day southern Iraq and the southeastern Arabian Peninsula, on the eastern shore of the Mediterranean Sea (Canaan), and in Africa. The descendants of Japheth are the brown, red, and yellow people. The brown people migrated into modern-day Greece, Macedonia, Tunis, Spain, Portugal, eastern Asia, and the islands off of Asia. Some brown people migrated into modern-day Alaska and down the coast of modern-day America and settled in North America, Central America, and South America. Those people who stopped in the area of Alaska are the Eskimos. They lived indoors out of the sun and ate fish, and their skin became yellow. Those who traveled south lived in the sun most of the time, became sunburned, and thus are Indians. Except for the Israelites, who were forbidden by God to intermarry with other tribes, there are various shades of coloring in people. The Israelites were commanded by God not to intermarry, and thus these are the fair and white people of the earth.

The Israelites are descendants of Shem, through Arphaxad and several others to Abram, changed to Abraham. There are many other branches of Shem's progeny who are not Israelites. Even Abraham had another son, Ishmael, whose descendants are not Israelites but are Arabs. God decreed that the Israelites would become as numerous as the sands of the seashore, so they would multiply greatly (Romans 9:27; Hosea 1:10; Genesis 22:17, 32:12). It is said by many in the United States that the white people in the United States are Gentiles, but that is not entirely true. Many of them are Gentiles. Most are

Israelites (Romans 9:26; Hosea 2:17; Isaiah 62:2, 65:15). (See exhibit 2 for the genealogy.) God said that Israelites would lose their identity. The new names given to them by God were Britain (British) and United States (American), and the name Israel would be a curse among them (Isaiah 65:15).

People don't seem to understand that God has a purpose for allowing the things that go on around the earth. The plagues that God put on Egypt so the pharaoh would let the Israelite people go should tell you a lot. God put several plagues on Egypt. You can read them in Exodus 8, 9, 10, and 11. One plague should have been enough for Pharaoh to let the Israelites go. But no! Each time God said he hardened the heart of Pharaoh and his people so that they would not let the Israelites go. Why? To show the people of all world history just what God could do and that he had a plan for earth. Every time you read those chapters, your knowledge of God and what he can do is reinforced. At the end-time some plagues will again be put on the earth to destroy those peoples and nations who will not conform to God's commandments.

God speaks to (charms) serpents, spiders, other animals, etc., so that they won't hurt his elect (Amos 9:3; Deuteronomy 8;15, 32:24; Jeremiah 8:17). God also stirs up humans and nations to do the work that needs to be done to carry out his plan for earth. People don't understand just why some things occur, but when Jesus returns to earth and sets up his world government, people will understand (Luke 10:19).

God created angels before he created human beings. Some of those angels inflated their importance, disobeyed God, and were thrown out of God's Kingdom (Revelation 12:7–9). Those castoffs, of whom Satan is chief, have been roaming the earth trying to convert anyone they can to evil ways and will continue to do so for a short time (I Peter 5:8). Satan is the god of this world now (II Corinthians 4:4).

God knows everything that is said and done and everything that enters into a person's mind (Ezekiel 11:5; Deuteronomy 23:14; II Samuel 14:20).

I recognized that there was a need for a brief summary of what has happened of importance to the United States and what will happen in the future. This book, written in 1989 and the first three months of 1990, tells it like it is, briefly, so anyone can understand his inheritance and destiny in one easy-to-understand book. God's covenant and inheritance with Israel (the United States and Great Britain) is everlasting (Ezekiel 16:60). The references used in writing this book are taken from the words of Jesus Christ, the disciples, and the prophets, instructions from God, as recorded in the Holy Bible, King James Version. (Please refer to exhibit 1 for a listing of who wrote the books of the Bible.) I urge all Israelites to read the Book of Genesis in the Bible over and over again. It tells you who you are.

Now to the revelation as to why the United States became the greatest single nation on earth and is Israel and what is going to happen to it.

Chapter 1 covers information as to who are the Israelites and why God chose them over other peoples for his inheritance. Chapter 2 shows how, with God's help, the United States came into being and rose to be the greatest nation on earth. Chapters 3 through 26 bare the twenty-four events that caused the destruction of the greatest nation on earth—the United States—and why it will go into captivity and decline. Chapter 27 is a brief summary of what will happen on earth just before Jesus returns to earth and what to expect when he does.

Knowledge has been shut up until the time of the end, and at the end-time of civilization as we know it knowledge will be revealed (Romans 11:8; Daniel 12:9; Revelation 22:10; Ephesians 3:5). The key to understanding is to know that the United States is Israel.

The Rise and Fall of the United States

Chapter I
The Israelites

In order to understand how and why the United States of America came into being, one has to go back to the time of Abraham, Isaac, and Jacob. The beginning of knowledge is to know that God has a plan for earth. Every major event that occurs is part of God's plan for earth (Genesis 1; Isaiah 45:4–18). You must recognize this before you can have understanding. Basically, God's plan is to allow human beings to create other human beings to be nurtured into healthy, intelligent, and morally satisfactory humans to God's high standards, to be permanent husbandmen of earth after the millennium unto eternity. Those humans who do not meet God's high standards will be destroyed.

After Adam and Eve sinned, God allowed Satan to roam the earth to test humans and convert those that he could to his evil ways. Even to this day, Satan is converting those that he can (Job 1:7; I Chronicles 16:22; Revelation 12:7–9), except that he cannot touch the elect. During the period from Adam to Noah everything became so evil on earth that God caused it to rain on the earth forty days and forty nights to destroy everything except Noah and his family and seven of every clean beast and of fowls and two of every unclean beast (Genesis 7:1–4). Noah and his family were the only righteous people acceptable to God on earth at that time. All was destroyed except for Noah and his family and the creatures that Noah took into the ark with him (Genesis 6:5–22, 7:21–23). Noah had three sons, namely, Shem, Ham, and Japheth, so all the population of the earth today comes from Noah and those three sons (Genesis 9:1). Trace your ancestry back to them if you can (Genesis 5:32). The descendants of Shem are the Semitic people; the descendants of Ham are the Hamitic (African) people; the descendants of Japheth are the Euro-Asiatic people.

The descendants of Shem are the white people of the earth; the descendants of Ham are the black people of the earth; and the descendants of Japheth are the brown, yellow, and red people of the earth.

Ham was the father of Canaan. The land of Canaan was where many of the Canaanites lived before the Israelites destroyed them or drove them out. Nimrod was of this tribe. Nimrod and his group occupied an area in southern Babylon that is modern-day Iraq. Ham and his descendants were cursed for all time because of an incident pointed out in Genesis 9:22–27. Because of this incident Ham and his descendants, the black peoples, even to this day, are relegated to be servants of Shem and his descendants and Japheth and his descendants. The descendants of Ham were giants (Deuteronomy 2:10–12, 19–23). It is estimated that some got to be as much as twelve feet tall. The descendants of Ham are not classified as Gentiles, and as they are not Israelites, they are classified as heathen (Genesis 10:6–20). They occupied the area of modern-day Israel for a time until vanquished. Many were killed by the Israelites and by the descendants of Esau. Some settled in an area of modern-day southern Iraq, in a southeastern part of the Arabian Peninsula, and on the island of Crete, and many migrated to Africa (Genesis 10:6–19; Numbers 13:32–33; Joshua 16:10).

Japheth and his descendants—the brown, yellow, and red people—were to grow in numbers and to be servants of Shem and his descendants even to this day (Genesis 9:25–27). The generations of Japheth (Genesis 10:2–5) scattered to central and eastern Asia and the islands off Asia and southern Europe. Those areas include China, Japan, India, southeast Asia, southern and eastern parts of the former USSR, Tarshish (which was an area in Spain and Portugal), Asia Minor, Bulgaria, Romania, Macedonia, Greece, Cyprus, Italy, Crete, Sicily, and Tunis. Some crossed the Bering Strait from Asia into Alaska and went down into North America, Central America, and South America. Those groups are the Indians and Eskimos of the Americas. Japheth's descendants are classified as Gentiles in Genesis 10:2–5.

The descendants of Shem are the white people of the world. They started out in modern-day Iraq, Syria, and the Arabian Peninsula and expanded worldwide from there (Genesis 10:21–32, 11:10–32). At the present time, they occupy most of the Arabian Peninsula, Asia Minor, Syria, Iraq, Lebanon, Jordan, Europe, the British Isles, the United States, Iran, Canada, Australia, South Africa, Iceland, the Falkland Islands, Pakistan, and Afghanistan.

The covenants and inheritances from God were to be for all time until the time of the end of civilization as we know it. All through history it has been that way—the black people have been servants to the white people and the brown people. Also, wherever the brown, red, and yellow people and the white people have been in the same area, the brown, red, and yellow people have been servants of the white people. It is no disgrace to be a servant or a slave. It is God's will. In an Israelite nation a stranger can be bought (Exodus 12:44). One that is bought by an Israelite can become one of Abraham's people and be saved, if he follows God's commandments. A hired stranger cannot become one of Abraham's people (Exodus

12:43–45). Considering this tenet, it appears that Abraham Lincoln made a gross error in his thinking and actions.

Originally, all peoples had one language (Genesis 11:1). God saw that because of this, they were getting too smart for their own good. The people were building the Tower of Babel to the heavens, so God confounded their language so that they could not understand each other's speech. He scattered them abroad the face of the earth (Genesis 11:4–9). As an aside for the benefit of modern-day scientists and world leaders, the heavens are God's secret and his home. With their modern-day electronic gadgets and devices they are creating a modern-day Tower of Babel and will be destroyed. With electronics all peoples can communicate with each other instantly. If these scientists and world leaders get more foolish and desire to explore outer space further, God will intervene to see that their projects come to nothing and destroy them. The billions of dollars being spent on these activities will be wasted.

God chose Abram, later changed to Abraham, to make his name great with many blessings and be a father of many nations (Genesis 22:15–18; Nehemiah 9:7–38). Abram was a white man (Genesis 11:10–32, 12:1–3, Genesis 17, 24:2–4; Acts 7:20; Nehemiah 9:8–38; Romans 4:13–17). Abram was promised all the land from the Nile River in Egypt to the Euphrates River in modern-day Iraq (Genesis 15:18–21). Abram, changed to Abraham, had a son named Ishmael by an Egyptian handmaid, Hagar, but this was not well received in the household by Sarah, Abram's wife. So Ishmael was sent into the wilderness (Genesis 16:4–12). His heritage was to multiply but not to be numbered for a multitude. His heritage was also to be a wild man and everyone would be against him and his descendants. Abram, changed to Abraham, had another son, named Isaac, by Sarah. With Isaac God established a covenant as a father of many nations (Genesis 17:5, 21).

Ishmael and his descendants dwelt in the wilderness, and Ishmael is the father of the Arab peoples (Genesis 21:21). These nations would include in addition to the Arabian Peninsula parts of northern Africa (Genesis 25:13–18).

Isaac, Abraham's heir, received the promise of many blessings, and his seed was to multiply "as the stars of the heaven and as the sand which is upon the seashore" (Genesis 22:17–19). His seed was to possess the gates of his enemies—gates such as Gibraltar, the Suez Canal, the Panama Canal, the Strait of Malacca, South Africa, the Falkland Islands, and Kattegat (Genesis 24:60). In his seed all nations of the earth would be blessed (Genesis 22:17–18).

When it was time for Isaac to take a wife, Abraham made the ruler of his household swear by the Lord, the God in Heaven and the God of the Earth, that he would not find a wife of the daughters of the Canaanites, who were the descendants of Ham, the black people, but would find a wife of his own kindred, the white people, for Isaac (Genesis 24:1–4). Rebekah was found for Isaac (Genesis 24:15–16, 60). Abraham gave all that he had to Isaac (Genesis 25:5) and nothing to Ishmael. Isaac prospered greatly (Genesis 26:12–15). Thus God's blessings to Abraham were passed on to Isaac (Genesis 26:2–5).

Isaac's wife, Rebekah, had two sons, namely, Esau and Jacob (Hebrews 11:20–21). The Lord said to Rebekah that she would bear twins and these would be the fathers of two great multitudes of people. One people would be stronger than the other people, and the elder would serve the younger. Esau, the older, was a cunning hunter, and Jacob, the younger, was a plain man that dwelled in tents and sold pottage (Genesis 25:22–29). Ordinarily Esau, the oldest son, would get the inheritance, but Esau sold his birthright for a mess of pottage from Jacob (Hebrews 12:16–17). Thus Esau gave up his birthright to Jacob (Genesis 25:29–34). Because of this God hated Esau (Romans 9:13; Malachi 1:3).

God, through Isaac, gave Jacob the blessing of "the dew of heaven, and the fatness of the earth, and plenty of corn and wine; let people serve thee and nations bow down to thee; be lord over thy brethren, and let thy mother's sons bow down to thee; cursed be every one that curseth thee, and blessed be he that blesseth you" (Genesis 27:28–29). This means that the Israelites will receive rain in due season, plenty of corn, wine, and good crops; and those people who are not Israelites will bow down to and serve the Israelites. Those that don't do this will be cursed, and those that do this will be blessed. Those are mighty strong words and an inheritance from God. The children of Jacob, whose name was later changed to Israel by God, and his descendants are God's chosen people forever (I Chronicles 16:13–17; Deuteronomy 32:8–14). They are protected and are to prosper greatly for all time (Isaiah 45:11–17). The Israelites are to be a special people separated from other people (Exodus 33:16; Leviticus 20:24). Israelites are to be given the choicest of lands.

Isaac charged Jacob, later changed to Israel, not to take a wife of the daughters of Canaan, the black people (Genesis 28:1). This was in order to continue the inheritance and blessing passed down from Abraham (Genesis 28:3–4).

The Lord God blessed Jacob, changed to Israel, to multiply greatly and to spread abroad to the west, to the east, to the north, and to the south, in the words the entire nation, "and all your families will be blessed; and your seed shall be as many as the dust of the earth'' (Genesis 28:13–15). Jacob's descendants are protected from the heathen forever (I Chronicles 16:15–36). Who are the Israelites? Jacob's descendants are the Israelites (Romans 9:4–13).

Jacob, changed to Israel, loved Rachel and took her for his wife, unto who Joseph was born. This is important because Joseph is the line of inheritance for the United States. Jacob had other sons by handmaids and another wife, Leah (Genesis 30:22–24). These are the sons of Jacob, whose name was changed to Israel:

By Rachel: Joseph and Benjamin
By Leah: Reuben, Simeon, Levi, Judah, Issachar, and Zebulon
By Bilhah: Dan and Naphtali
By Zilpah: Gad and Asher

You will note that there are twelve sons (Genesis 35:23–26).

Jacob wrestled with an angel of God, to a draw, whereupon the angel of God blessed Jacob and changed his name from Jacob to Israel (Genesis 32:24–32, 35:10). The Israelites are God's chosen people forever and ever (II Samuel 7:16, 24, 29; I Chronicles 16:13–17, 17:22–27; Romans 9:13). Jacob loved Joseph more than all his other children, because he was the son of his old age and also because he was the son of Rachel, Jacob's true love. Because Israel (formerly Jacob) loved Joseph the most, the other sons hated Joseph (Genesis 37:3–4). Joseph was to have dominion over his brothers (Genesis 37:6–8). The other sons conspired to kill Joseph; however, Reuben objected (Genesis 37:13–21), so they agreed to sell Joseph to a company of Ishmaelites who were journeying to Egypt, and they did so (Genesis 37:22–36). They told Israel that Joseph had been killed.

Reuben was the firstborn of Israel, but he defiled his father's bed, so the birthright was given to Joseph (Genesis 49:3–4; I Chronicles 5:1). Judah prevailed above his brothers and was chief ruler (I Chronicles 5:2). This may have been because he was the biggest, spoke the loudest, and was the most aggressive, but we don't know for sure. Some of these characteristics are noted in the tribe of Judah even as of this date. You will note that Reuben was the one who had compassion for Joseph, and even to this day Reuben's descendants, now living in France, have brotherly feelings toward Joseph's descendants, now living in the United States and Great Britain. You will also note that the primary instigator to kill Joseph, amended to selling Joseph into captivity, was Judah, now the modern-day nation that calls itself Israel and who even now as of this date is trying to take advantage of Joseph's descendants, the United States and Great Britain. As an aside, the nation that calls itself Israel today is misnamed. It is actually Judah. At the end-time when all the tribes of Israel are assembled back at Jerusalem, then it rightly can be called Israel.

Because of his actions, Judah apparently felt guilty, or perhaps he was harassed out of the family circle, but anyway, Judah left his brothers and married a Canaanite, a descendant of the black people, and had many difficulties (Genesis 38).

After Joseph was carried away to Egypt, he was well thought of in Egypt and prospered and received many favors (Genesis 39–41). Joseph married in Egypt and had two sons, namely, Manasseh, the descendants of whom are now the United States, and Ephraim, the descendants of whom are now Great Britain, Canada, Australia, and partially South Africa (Genesis 41:50–52). Later on, Joseph brought his father, Israel, and his brothers to Egypt to prosper along with him.

When Israel was old and about to die, he called Joseph's sons, Ephraim and Manasseh, to him and passed on his blessings and inheritance. Manasseh received a blessing to become a great nation, a multitude in the midst of the earth, which is the United States, and Ephraim received a blessing to become a greater multitude of nations, which is the British Empire (Genesis 48).

Israel also called together his other sons to tell them of their inheritance (Genesis 49). In the last days here is where the tribes of Israel are located:

Reuben—	France and Belgium Will have dignity and power but will be unstable. Reuben defiled his father's bed, so even though as the firstborn he ordinarily would have the birthright, it was taken away from him and given to Joseph (I Chronicles 5:1).
Zebulon—	the Netherlands and Belgium They will dwell in a haven of the sea.
Asher—	Norway, Sweden, Denmark, Iceland, and Finland They will produce good food and royal dainties.
Naphtali—	Switzerland and Austria Will have good music and writings and be energetic.
Issachar—	Germany and Luxembourg Will be strong but have two burdens (East and West Germany) Will suppress its wrongdoing and will pay others because of wrongdoing.

Dan—	Ireland Will bite his brothers as a serpent and will fall back and lose their inheritance. Note Dan's terroristic activity.
Judah—	scattered among all the nations of the earth Will be taken captive and will be a curse among the heathen. Will have many enemies and will strive against them. People will look to Judah for instruction concerning religious matters, as they are the keeper of the sceptre (the commandments of God). They will commit many transgressions (I Chronicles 1:2; Jeremiah 13:19–25, 16, 17:1–4; Zechariah 8:13; Nehemiah 11:4).
Benjamin—	scattered among all the nations of the earth along with Judah Like a raving wolf will devour others and will prosper. (Jeremiah 13:19–25, 16, 17:1–4; Nehemiah 11:4).
Levi—	scattered among all the tribes of Israel and other nations Will be angry and cruel men and secretive. Will handle religious matters (Numbers 1:47–53, 8:13–26).
Simeon—	scattered among all the tribes of Israel Will be angry, cruel, and secretive men.
Gad—	Estonia and Hungary Will be overcome but will break out to freedom at end-time.
Joseph:	Manasseh—the United States Ephraim—Great Britain, Canada, and Australia

The birthright was given to Joseph and his sons (I Chronicles 5:1). In accordance with inheritance from God these people will prosper greatly, have bountiful harvests, have good health, and be secure from their enemies. They will multiply greatly.

These are the twelve tribes of Israel that God chose as *his* people (Jeremiah 31:1; I Chronicles 17:21–22). You will note that Joseph is split into two tribes. However, the tribe of Levi has no inheritance (Joshua 13:14; Numbers 18:23–24). Thus when we speak of inheritance there are just twelve tribes. Also, at the time of the end when the tribes are assembled back into Jerusalem for their salvation, the tribe of Dan is not included, but the tribe of Levi is included (Revelation 7:4–8). When we speak of salvation, there are still only twelve tribes.

The children of Israel lived, multiplied, and prospered in Egypt many years. The Israelites were oppressed by the Egyptians and prayed to God for help. God picked Moses to lead the Israelites out of Egypt, to lands that God directed them to (Exodus 12, 13:5, 14, 19:3–6; Numbers 31:1–18, 32:32–33, 34:1–2). Moses was very fair, that is, light-complexioned and possibly with blond hair. In other words, he was white (Acts 7:20). Moses was of the tribe of Levi (Exodus 2:1–3). He was a very meek person (Numbers 12:3). God ordinarily speaks through dreams to prophets. Moses was a reluctant prophet, and God spoke directly to Moses (Exodus 7:1). Thus Moses, with God's instructions, led the Israelites out of captivity in Egypt to a land promised to them. During the forty-year period of the exodus from Egypt many Israelites changed and believed not in God and thus were killed (Jude 1:5; Joshua 5:4–7). All those twenty years of age and over except Caleb and Joshua and the Levites (Numbers 14:26–30) died.

God made a covenant with the children of Israel (Exodus 19:3–6, 34:27–28) to be in effect forever (Isaiah 59:21). They are to prosper, to multiply greatly, and to be protected from their enemies (Genesis 28:14; Isaiah 41:11–14). The Israelites are to be a special people, separated from other people (Exodus 33:16; Leviticus 20:24). Israelites are to be given the choicest of lands. The children of Israel can be identified at any time and any place by those peoples that follow the Ten Commandments (Exodus 20:1–17). Also, they are fair-complexioned (Acts 7:20). Another identifying mark is their ability to blush (Jeremiah 6:15). They are blessed for all time (Numbers 6:22–27; I Kings 8:53).

No nation can stand up to a nation of Israel (Isaiah 54:15–17; Deuteronomy 28:7). The tribes of Israel are protected from the heathen forever (I Chronicles 16:20–25, 35–36; Deuteronomy 4:5–8). Unless, of course, the tribes or a tribe of Israel turn their back on the Ten Commandments, which happened at one time back when Assyria took Israel captive, which also happened to the nation of Judah. If non-Israelites enter into a land of Israel, they are to be laborers or overseers of laborers. They are not to be rulers, administrators, or managers (I Chronicles 22:2–4; II Chronicles 2:17–18, 8:7–9; Joshua 9:4–27.

God commanded the tribes of Israel that wherever they go into heathen nations and take them over they are to utterly destroy them and their works (Deuteronomy 7:1–6; I Chronicles 17:21–23). If any heathen were left alive, they were to be bondsmen and slaves (I Kings 9:20–21). No heathen works or activities are allowed to remain or to be followed within an Israelite nation. When an Israelite nation defeats a heathen nation, if Israel does not take over the land, then it is an abomination to then build it up by granting it loans, money, gifts, etc. That is why it is an abomination for the United States (Israel) to build up Japan, Korea, southeast Asia, or any other nation that fought the United States in any of its wars. Israel, under David, conquered all those heathen nations in the area that he wanted to conquer (I Chronicles 18, 20). It is all right for an Israelite nation to assist another Israelite nation. It is perfectly proper to assist those nations listed in a previous paragraph as where Israelites are located. South Africa, for example, is considered Israelite because it is ruled by Israelites from Great Britain, Germany, Holland, and France. Thus it would be perfectly proper for the United States to assist South Africa in its troubles. If it should happen that South Africa would be taken over by a heathen people, then it would be an abomination for the United States to help them. If the Israelites in South Africa turn their back on God, then South Africa could fall into the hands of the heathen.

With regards to the Israelites, God decides who goes where and who is to prosper and who is not to prosper (Deuteronomy 32:8–9).

Because there has been considerable intermarriage over the centuries and tribal movement, along with the fact that country or nation boundaries may encompass more than one tribe or many tribes, groups or tribes may have lost their identity. There might even be isolated groups of Israelites located in Gentile and heathen nations. Those areas that are not considered to be Israelite are all of Asia except the nation that calls itself Israel today, all of Africa except South African white areas, all of South America, all of Central America and Mexico, all of the islands except the Falkland Islands, Iceland, the British Isles, and other small islands around northern and western Europe, and all of the rest of Europe except those nations listed in a previous paragraph showing where the various tribes of Israel are located. Hawaii is not Israelite. The annexation of Hawaii was an abomination and completely wrong.

The descendants of Ishmael, the second son of Abraham, and Esau, the other son of Isaac, are from the lineage of Shem and thus considered white people if they did not intermarry with tribes who were descendants of Ham or Japheth. But they are not Israelites. Also, the other sons of Shem and their descendants can be considered white people provided that they did not intermarry with tribes who were descendants of Ham or Japheth. Also, Abraham took another wife, Keturah, who gave Abraham several sons (Genesis 25:1–4). These can be considered white people. Those people who settled in the Arabian Peninsula, Asia Minor, Greece, Italy, Spain, northern Africa, Portugal, Iran, Iraq, Afghanistan, Syria, western India, Pakistan, and eastern Europe (except Estonia, Latvia, and Lithuania) are not Israelites. Some Israelites were briefly in those areas but moved on to northern and western Europe. Understandably, the descendants of Ham and Japheth are not Israelites.

The Israelites had strict, God-imposed rules about marriage outside of their tribes. A marriage or union by an Israelite outside of his tribe resulted in children who are mongrels up to a tenth generation, who shall not enter into the congregation of the Lord (Deuteronomy 23:2). There is evidence that the word *bastard* in the Bible was mistranslated and should be *mongrel* or *half-breed*. It makes no difference if they are married or not married. Because the offspring are mongrels, they cannot be Israelites. It would take ten generations for descendants to become "clean" and acceptable into the congregation of the Lord, provided that no one during that time introduced another heathen or Gentile into the line. The term *bastard* as related to the dictionary definition as opposed to the Bible use does not make sense. If two Israelites are not married in accordance with modern-day society's definition of marriage but have a child, the child is undoubtedly an Israelite, provided that there are no sexual relations with anyone else. I don't believe that there were marriage ceremonies back in Abraham's time (Genesis 12:10–19, 20:1–4). *Mongrels* is the correct term for children of an Israelite and a non-Israelite, regardless of whether the parents are married by modern-day standards or not married.

Esau took a wife who was a daughter of Ishmael, Abraham's son (Genesis 28:9). In addition, Esau had many wives from Canaan, the black peoples (Genesis 36:1–43), and a wife who was a Hittite (Genesis 26:34–35). Esau was a hairy man who loved to hunt (Genesis 25:25–27). His descendants are mostly located in the area now of Turkey, Greece, Italy, Spain, Iran, Portugal, the Balkans, South America, Central America, and Mexico. There was probably much intermarrying in the early times between Esau's descendants, Ishmael's descendants, Ham's descendants, and Japheth's descendants, but not with Jacob's descendants (changed to Israel) because God forbid it. Those few descendants of Jacob who might have married into other tribes through ignorance would lose their inheritance.

God chose Abraham, Isaac, Jacob (changed to Israel), Joseph, and their descendants to be a special people, because God loved them. He made a covenant with them (Deuteronomy 7:6–8). If the Israelite nations keep the Ten Commandments, they will be blessed beyond all their wildest dreams, and any nation that opposes them will be destroyed (Deuteronomy 7:11–26, Exodus 33:16; Leviticus 20:24).

The people of Israel took over many lands and cities with God's help. The Israelites, with God's blessing, drove out or killed all the people of the lands that they took over, such as Canaan (Joshua 3:10, 6:20–24, 8:18–29, 9:24–27, 10, 11, 12:1–24, 13:1–33, 23:10–11, 24:1–26; I Samuel 17:41–53, II Samuel 10:17–19; I Chronicles 4:40–43, 5:10–22, 14:8–17, 18:11–13, 19:16–19). In at least one instance a few Canaanites were allowed to remain as slaves (Joshua 16:9–10). But in many instances all men, women, and children were killed.

Israelites are not to adopt any of the customs or make marriages with any of the peoples of the nations that are not Israelites (Joshua 23:11–17; Exodus 33:16; Deuteronomy 7:3). If they do, they lose their inheritance (Judges 3:1–8; Jeremiah 2:21, 25). Israelites who marry outside their tribes are rejected, and their children are mongrels to the tenth generation (Deuteronomy 23:2; Jude 7; Hosea 5:6–7). It is understood that the word *bastard* in the Bible is translated from the Hebrew word *manzer*, which means "a mixture, half-breed or mongrel."

The colored tribes of Canaan whom the Israelites destroyed, taking over their lands, were giants (Joshua 12:4; Numbers 13:32–33). Some were estimated to be twelve feet tall. This destruction of Canaan was because of God's plan for the inheritance of his chosen people, Israel. When God brought them out of Egypt he promised them the choicest of lands. Judah was assigned by God to destroy the Canaanites. Judah got Simeon to accompany him to do this job. The other tribes of Israel did not drive out the Canaanites, the Jebusites, the Hittites, and other heathen but made them slaves (Judges 1). But Judah did the job assigned to him.

Earlier Judah had left his brethren and taken a Canaanite, of the black people, as a wife (Genesis 38). As a result Judah had all kinds of troubles and apparently lost favor with God. Some black peoples claim that they are Israelites. It is possible that these claimants are descendants of that union. Also, most of those of the tribe of Judah have a darker skin than the other Israelites.

Israelites who marry non-Israelites are condemned (Nehemiah 13:23–27) and should not associate with non-Israelites (Nehemiah 13).

After many years, there developed differences of ideology between groups of the tribes of Israel. They split into two groups (Jeremiah 31:31, 36:2). The ten tribes of Ephraim, Manasseh, Reuben, Dan, Gad, Zebulon, Issachar, Asher, Naphtali, and Simeon joined together in Samaria and called themselves Israel (I Kings 11:28–31; Jeremiah 31:31–36). The tribes of Judah and Benjamin joined together into the nation of Judah with headquarters at Jerusalem (Nehemiah 11:4; I Kings 12). Most of Levi stayed with them (Nehemiah 11:15). There was war between the two houses or nations (II Samuel 3:1). Saul was the leader of the ten Israel tribes, and David was the chief ruler over Judah (II Samuel 3:1–10), 24:1). Probably the most difficult times between the two nations was when Rehoboam was king of Judah and Jeroboam was king of Israel at Samaria (I Kings 14, 15).

Thus Israel and Judah are two separate nations. Many people think that Judah (the Jews) are God's chosen people. That is not true. Israel is God's chosen people (Jeremiah 31:31–33). The Jews rejected Jesus and his words (Acts 13:44–46; John 5:15-47) and had him killed (John 18, 19; Matthew 12:14; Mark 3:6; John 11:47–53). Jesus was sent to the lost sheep of the house of Israel (Matthew 15:24), and Jesus commissioned his disciples to go to the lost sheep of the house of Israel, which were the ten tribes of Israel that were originally at Samaria and were later taken captive by the Assyrians just before the time Jesus was on the earth. The Assyrians were located in present-day Iraq and northwest Iran.

While at Samaria, the people of the nation of Israel did bad things and did not follow the Ten Commandments. This made God angry, so Assyria (a heathen nation) was allowed to take Israel captive (II Kings 17:1–12). Assyria took the Israelite people over to the area between the Black Sea and Caspian Sea, an area that is in northern Iraq, northwest Iran, and southern Russia. This is where the Caucasian Mountains are located (II Kings 18:9–12). The Assyrians were later absorbed by the Medes, then the Persians. There was probably much intermarriage between different peoples in those days.

The Israelites kept to themselves, multiplied greatly, and expanded into modern-day Iran, Pakistan, western India, Afghanistan, northern Asia Minor, and southern parts of the former USSR. Years later, the Israelites migrated from these areas and the Caucasian Mountains north and west to northern and western Europe. (See exhibit 4.) Later, many migrated to the United States, Canada, Australia, and South Africa. Even to this day, or at least until the Gentiles and heathen got control of the affairs in Washington and passed the antidiscrimination laws, when a person filled out an application for anything, there was a question on the form such as "Are you Caucasian?" This shows that the early immigrants to the United States recognized their ancestry and inheritance.

At the time of Israel's captivity, Judah was protected by God from the Assyrians (II Kings 19:32–37) for King David's sake. Later on Judah went to whoredoms and other abominations and was allowed to be taken captive by the Babylonians, who were located in present-day southern Iraq.

Another sidelight of the captivity of the Israelites was that the Assyrians moved some of their own people into the area of Samaria vacated by the Israelites. The Assyrians were heathen and had much trouble in the land of Samaria. Some were eaten by lions (II Kings 17:24–25). They were not capable of taking care of the land like the Israelites did. This showed that God did not approve of them but nevertheless allowed them to take Israel captive, to shake Israel up and teach Israel a lesson. Samaria had been God's land, but the Assyrians did not know how to take care of it and do evil things even to this day—now (II Kings 17:26–34, 41). Samaria is an area including Lebanon north of the present-day nation of Israel. With all the turmoil in that area now, it is Bible prophecy being fulfilled.

Later on, the nation of Judah did things that displeased God, so Babylon was allowed to take Judah captive and to destroy Jerusalem (II Kings 21:11–15, 24:10–16, II Kings 25; Jeremiah 11:9–14,13:6–25, 19:4–15, 25:11–12; II Chronicles 36). Only a few were allowed to remain in the area of Jerusalem.

In 701 B.C., the cities of Judah were destroyed by Sennacherib of Assyria. Judah was subservient to Assyria until 625 B.C., when Josiah came to power. Babylon, which was a part of Assyria, revolted and took control of Assyria about 625 B.C.. Assyria had let Jerusalem stand; however, Babylon then captured Jerusalem in 597 B.C., and most of the people and things in Jerusalem of value were deported to Babylon. A puppet was set up in Jerusalem, who later rebelled against Babylon. In 587 B.C. Jerusalem and all remaining vestiges of Judah were destroyed and the rest of the people were taken captive of Babylon. Thus Judah ended as a nation.

In 538 B.C., the Babylonians allowed the Jews (Judah) to return to the Jerusalem area, but only a few did return. A few years later, under a more compassionate King Darius, more Jews returned and the temple at Jerusalem was rebuilt, the walls of Jerusalem restored, and the laws of the

Bible reestablished, such as the sabbaths and prohibition against mixed marriages.

Other Bible references concerning the destruction of Judah are Jeremiah, 29:10, 39:8–10, 52:15–16; Nehemiah 1:3; II Kings 25:1–12; Ezra 1:1–3, 2:1–61, 4:12, 5:1.

While Judah was captive in Babylon and mixed with the Babylonians, apparently some religious leaders of Judah developed what is called the "Judeo-Christian" theme, which is also popular today. This was espoused by the Pharisees and the Sadducees. Jesus condemned it (Mark 8:15; Matthew 5:20, 23:13–29; Luke 11:39).

After the remnant of Judah returned to Jerusalem, the people of Judah were referred to for the first time as "Jews." These were the people of the tribes of Judah, Benjamin, and Levi. While living as captives in Babylon, the people of the tribes of Judah and Benjamin adopted some ideas contrary to the true Hebrew tenets of Moses' time. Thus there came into being the Pharisees and Sadducees. These were the Jews who persecuted God's true people and killed Jesus. Jesus condemned them (Matthew 3:7, 15:1–9). The authority for Judaism is the Talmud, which had its beginning in Babylon and is somewhat different from the religion of Moses' time. Judaism is followed by the Jews even to this day.

The ten tribes of Israel have become lost in history until the time of the end—now. The nation of Israel was referred to as "the lost ten tribes of Israel." Actually, many people knew where they were. Jesus' apostles knew where they were, because Jesus commanded the apostles to go to preach to the lost tribes of Israel. Where the apostles went shows you at that time in history where the lost tribes of Israel were located. (See exhibit 3 as to where the apostles went.) They were called lost because they had turned away from the Ten Commandments and unless the apostles could bring them back to observing the Ten Commandments they would lose their salvation and inheritance. At the end-time, the true identity of the Israelites will be revealed. Israel as a nation will be resurrected. Knowledge has been sealed up until the time of the end (Daniel 12:9).

After the remnant of Judah returned to Jerusalem from Babylon, they returned to their abominations and had problems with the heathen tribes in the area, so Judah, Benjamin, and Levi left Jerusalem and scattered to other areas and nations, all over the world (II Kings 19:30–31; Jeremiah 16:1–13, 17:1–4). Judah was worse than Israel, so Judah was scattered by God to all the nations of the earth, including heathen nations (Jeremiah 3:8–11, 5:11, Jeremiah 16–17). Jerusalem became a desolate place (Jeremiah 9; Isaiah 65:2–7). There was nothing Judah could do about it, because God willed it. Jerusalem was God's holy city, and at the end-time Jerusalem will be rebuilt into a grand and holy city. It will be the new world headquarters occupied by the elect (Isaiah 65:17–25). The tribe of Judah was designated by God as the lawgivers, keeping the tenets of the Bible and the Ten Commandments given to Moses, and all through history people looked to Judah for answers pertaining to God and God's commandments. Remember Israel has become lost until the time of the end, so no one looked to them. Israel and Judah both did evil things, but Judah more so than Israel, and thus Judah got the worse punishment (Jeremiah 3:11, 11:9–14) and was scattered to all the nations because of it. The tribe of Judah was chosen by God to be the spiritual ruler over all Israel (all twelve tribes), and David and his sons were to be kings. At the resurrection, David will resume rulership (I Chronicles 28:1–5). God loved David and his love passed on to his son, Solomon. As an example of God's thinking,

Solomon only asked God for wisdom and knowledge, and because that is all he asked for, he was given many blessings (II Chronicles 1:9–12).

The Jews, who were scattered to all the nations of the world (Ezekiel 22), including heathen nations, because they failed to follow God's commandments (Nehemiah 1:8), will be allowed by God to return to Jerusalem if they change their ways (Nehemiah 1:9). At the end-time, now, many are returning to Jerusalem.

There will always be a throne of David. Historians have stated that this throne is in England (tribe of Ephraim) now and has been for many years (Jeremiah 33:17). Probably Jeremiah took it with him when he escaped from Jerusalem. There had to be some in Judah who retained and obeyed the tenets and commandments of the Bible. Perhaps only a handful. These people would be the true Hebrews. These people would be in David's line in order to carry on God's will that there would always be a "throne of David." God would not allow any of the Judeo-Christian sect to occupy the throne of David. The Judeo-Christian sect was started by the Pharisees and the Sadducees after they came out of Babylon.

David was of the tribe of Judah (I Chronicles 2:3–15). Note the name Pharez. This continues the line to David. Also note the name Boaz and how it ties into the Book of Ruth in the Bible. The Pharez, Boaz, David, and descendants' line is the Davidic "throne of David" line, which God eternalized even as of this date and unto eternity. This line is now in England.

Lot was an Israelite and a righteous man (Genesis 11:27, 31, Genesis 19). However, he did wrong. The Ammonites and the Moabites came from the offspring of Lot and his two daughters, which was incest (Genesis

19:36–38). Sometimes God forgives indiscretions after generations have passed. Note in the Book of Ruth in the Bible how Ruth, a Moabitess, became the wife of Boaz and thus became a part of the Davidic line.

God's commandments are strict. Bastards and descendants of bastards are to be excluded from Israel forever (Nehemiah 13:1–3; Deuteronomy 23:2–3). Bastards are defined as the offspring of Israelites with non-Israelites, regardless of whether marriage was involved or not. They are mongrels, and any such are to be excluded up to the tenth generation (Deuteronomy 23:2). This probably means forever, because mongrels tend to associate with other mongrels and Israelites are forbidden to marry or have sexual relations with a mongrel. This is not the same situation as occurred with Lot.

The tribe of Levi was chosen by God to be the priests to handle all church matters, the house of the Lord, and the Ark of the covenant. Moses was of the tribe of Levi. They had no inheritance and other Israelites contributed tithes to support them (I Chronicles 23; Nehemiah 10:37–38; Numbers 1:47–53, 3:31–32). After Israel got into trouble with God, the tribe of Levi went with Judah and Benjamin. This group comprised the nation of Judah. After Judah was taken into captivity by Babylon, a remnant of Judah escaped to Egypt, where many died (Jeremiah 43:5–7, 44:12–14). Jeremiah and a few followers made their way to Ireland. This small group that went to Ireland was undoubtedly a few members of the nation of Judah who had kept the commandments of God, including one member of King David's line (Ruth 4:18–22; Jeremiah 44:28). Historians say that a princess of King David's line of descendants accompanied Jeremiah to Ireland. The princess had married previously a member of royalty from Ireland who was a descendant of Zarah, a son of Judah.

The descendants of this union first ruled in Ireland; then the throne was overturned and they ruled in Scotland; then it was overturned again, and they rule in England to this day. Thus God's decree that David's throne will continue until Jesus returns holds true. (See exhibit 5 for the lineage pertaining to David's Throne.)

When Jesus returns to earth the second time, this throne will be reset at Jerusalem. Jesus will rule the world from there and David will be resurrected as a king and rule with Jesus (Ezekiel 37:24; Acts 2:29–39; II Samuel 7:16). When Jesus established God's new world order of things the first time he came to earth, the Levites faded into obscurity and they became part of Jewish society (Numbers 18).

One of the commandments of God was that the people of Israel must not take strange wives or husbands; that means those people that are not of the tribes of Israel. The penalty was exclusion or even death (Nehemiah 10:28–30; Hosea 1:2–9, 5:3–7; Ezra 9, 10:1–44). Thus the Israelites are a clannish group of people. For example, the Reubenites stuck together and can now be located mostly in France. The same for the other tribes. That is why you can pinpoint the tribes down to a specific country or countries or area. Those people in earlier times knew of their inheritance, and despite their rebellion against the commandments, they remained together with God's help. The tribes of Judah, Levi, and Benjamin were the only tribes that were scattered, and because God willed it there was nothing that they could do about it.

The lost ten tribes of Israel that had backslidden and were allowed to be taken captive by the Assyrians apparently saw the error of their ways, returned to God's commandments with help from the apostles, kept together, and escaped from the Caucasian Mountain area to northern and western Europe and took over heathen areas with God's help. Later many migrated to Canada, the United States, Australia, and South Africa and took over those heathen areas with God's help.

While Judah was commissioned to keep the law of Moses and the oracles of God (Romans 3:1–2) and dispense them to the world, grace and truth were dispensed to the lost ten tribes by Jesus and his disciples (John 1:17). Jesus sent the apostles to preach to the lost ten tribes of Israel, and Israel returned again to the principles and commandments of God. They never went back to Samaria, because that area had been taken over by the heathen. Those ten tribes were the white peoples who migrated to northern Europe, western Europe, the British Isles, including Ireland, and Iceland. Their paths can be followed by the names given to various places. Jesus said that he was sent by God to the lost sheep of the house of Israel. Other peoples were called dogs (Matthew 15:21–28; Revelation 22:15; Philippians 3:2).

The people of Israel have forgotten who they are because God gave them a new name—Americans and British (Isaiah 62:2, 65:15; Hosea 2:17). At the end-time, the Israelites will be instructed as to who they are and reunited into a new nation of Israel at Jerusalem (Hosea 1:4–11).

A key point in determining whether you are an Israelite or not is the matter of God's commandment to marry only within the Israelite tribes (Numbers 36:8–9). An Israelite should not marry or have any sexual relations with a non-Israelite. If any Israelite marries or has sexual relationships with anyone outside the tribes of Israel, then he loses his inheritance of prosperity, good health, safety from his enemies, etc. Also, there is a further restriction regarding marriage in that members of a tribe are to marry only another member of the same tribe (Numbers 27:6–11, 36:3). The tribes were given different inheritances by God, and if any married outside of their tribe they would lose their inheritance for that tribe.

Jesus said that he was sent only to the lost sheep of the house of Israel (the lost ten tribes). He did not approve of other peoples (Matthew 15:24–27). The genealogy of Jesus back to Adam is in Luke 3:23–38. Jesus sent his disciples to the lost sheep of the house of Israel. Jesus' apostles were not educated men, except Judas, so apparently they were not fluent speakers, just ordinary working folks.

There are many other white peoples that are not Israelites. Abraham took another wife, Keturah, who had six sons and many descendants. These are considered white people but not Israelites (Genesis 25:1–8). Also, there are the descendants of Ishmael and Esau. Ishmael's descendants settled in the Arabian Peninsula and are the Arab people. Through intermarriage with the brown and black people, we can see where the descendants can have different shades of coloring. Areas where these peoples are now located, in addition to the Arabian Peninsula, are Iraq, Jordan, Lebanon, Syria, parts of Iran, Ethiopia, and northern Africa. Esau was a hairy hunter. The descendants of Esau probably occupy Spain, Italy, Greece, the Balkans, Iran, Pakistan, parts of India, Afghanistan, eastern Europe, Portugal, parts of Egypt, parts of northern Africa, parts of Asia Minor, parts of Central America and Mexico, and parts of South America. Some of the Israelites that went into captivity in the area of the Caucasian Mountains may have backslidden and intermarried with some of the Assyrians. Some of this mixture probably migrated along with the Israelites into Europe. Likely areas where this mixture is located are in eastern Europe, such as Romania, Bulgaria, Czechoslovakia, Poland, Yugoslavia, parts of Germany, and parts of Russia. I cannot believe that God would have allowed any group of Israelites to become part of a communist area or system, at least for long. Israelites would never accept being in an area where they could not worship God, nor would God permit it. The Assyrians had customs God did not approve of, and some of those customs undoubtedly were brought with them when they migrated into Europe. As an aside, looking into the decision of the Catholic Church to bring the eastern Europeans into the Catholic Church, I understand that one of the conditions of acceptance was that the Catholic Church had to accept and adopt some of those customs.

Many Gentiles are Christians but are not Israelites. They have a form of religion but do not follow all of God's Ten Commandments. They are more caught up in rituals and procedures than doing the will of God. The Israelites are to be the light of the Gentiles (Isaiah 49:6, 54:3, 60:3). Those people who were not of the house of Israel were called dogs by Jesus (Matthew 15:22–26), but he had compassion for them on occasion.

Paul, who originally was a Pharisee (Romans 11:1, I Corinthians 15:9) and who is considered an apostle by many, was not one of the original apostles. He was a Jew of the tribe of Benjamin (Philippians 3:5) who persecuted the Israelites but later converted to God's principles. He was sent to preach to the Gentiles (Romans 11:13, 15:16). So wherever Paul went we know that those peoples were Gentiles. Paul went to southern Asia Minor, to Greece, to Italy, and to Spain, so we know that those peoples are Gentiles and not Israelites. He was rejected in many places, especially by the Jews in those places (Acts 18:4–6, 21:20–40; I Corinthians 12:2; Romans 1:14–15, 15:28). Those

Jews that rejected the teaching of Paul were judged unworthy of everlasting life (Acts 13:45–46). Paul is buried in England.

The Jews rejected and persecuted Christ's disciples (Acts 12:1–3, 11). Because they did not follow Christ's teaching, the Jews were scattered by God to all the nations of the earth and suffered persecutions (I Thessalonians 2:14–16). Jerusalem became desolate because of that. The Jews, despite their abominations that caused their scattering to all the nations of the earth (Zechariah 7:14), received some special consideration from God because the oracles of God were committed to them (Romans 3:1–2). The oracles of God are the commandments of God (Hebrews 5:12). Jesus said that salvation is of the Jews (John 4:22), because they were to keep the oracles of God, in other words, to keep the knowledge of God's words and to dispense and publicize those words to all those peoples who wanted to know. Jesus was from the tribe of Judah, as were his apostles. Those Apostles were commanded to go preach salvation to the lost tribes of Israel. The lost tribes were lost in the sense that they had turned away from God's commandments and done evil things, and thus they would lose their inheritance and salvation unless they turned around and returned to God's commandments.

The first covenant given to Moses and maintained by the Levitical priesthood was abolished by Jesus, and Jesus made a new covenant to be preached by the apostles (Hebrews 8:6–10). The main things that were changed by Jesus were doing away with the animal sacrifices, the rituals, and circumcision (I Corinthians 7:18–19). The Ten Commandments were retained and in fact reinforced. When Jesus sacrificed himself on the cross, that took the place of the animal sacrifices that had been commanded previously. It also altered the significance of the Levitical priesthood.

All nations and peoples that do not worship Jesus Christ are heathen. Babylon was heathen (Lamentations 1:3). In times prior to Jesus, those who adopted strange gods or did not believe in God were heathen. Paul for a short time preached to the heathen (Galatians 1:16–17), but his commission was to preach to the Gentiles. Gentiles and heathen can become saved by accepting Jesus Christ and by following the Ten Commandments (Galatians 3). The Gentile and heathen areas of the world are South America, Central America, Mexico, Africa (except white South Africa), Asia (except the nation that calls itself Israel today), eastern Europe (except Estonia, Latvia, and Lithuania), almost all the islands of the world (except the British Isles, the Falkland Islands, and Iceland). Assyria, which took Israel captive, was part of modern-day northern Iraq and northwest Iran. Babylon, which took Judah captive, was part of modern-day southern Iraq. The Assyrians are descendants mainly of Esau and were originally also in the area of Babylon, but in A.D. 637 the Arabs, descendants of Ishmael, drove the Persians (previously called Assyrians) out of the area. So that area is now controlled by the Arab people. The descendants of Ham are the black people. Many occupied Canaan until the Israelites, with God's help, destroyed them and took over the area. Some of Ham's descendants settled in southern Babylon and the southeastern Arabian Peninsula, but the majority settled in Africa. The northern nations of Africa are undoubtedly peopled by the descendants of Ishmael, Esau, Ham, and Japheth, a mixture, with much intermarriage. Because of biblical reference to it at the time of the end captivity of Israel, it appears that Egypt is also considered Assyrian.

The lost sheep of the house of Israel (the lost ten tribes of Israel) were taken captive by the Assyrians and taken over to an area between the Caspian Sea and the Black Sea in what is now northwest Iran and southern Russia in 721 B.C.. This is the area of the Caucasian Mountains. This was permitted by God because the ten tribes in Samaria had fallen away from God's commandments. While in captivity, they grew in numbers and spread out into what is now western India, Afghanistan, northern Iraq, northern Turkey, Iran, and southern, parts of the former USSR. Over the centuries, many of these people lost track of their true identity, and as of this date many do not know that they are true Israelites. Most think that they are Gentiles. Those peoples moved from those locations to Europe later.

To prove the location and identity of those Israelites, one needs only to look to where the twelve apostles went. Jesus commanded the apostles to go to the lost sheep of the house of Israel. (Please see exhibit 3 as to where the apostles went.)

The apostles were not to preach to the Jews, nor to the Gentiles, nor to the heathen. Note Matthew 10:5–6: "These twelve Jesus sent forth, and commanded them, saying 'Go not into the way of the Gentiles, and into any city of the Samaritans enter ye not; but go rather to the lost sheep of the house of Israel.' " The Jews, who were the Pharisees and Sadducees, had rejected Jesus (Matthew 3:7). The Gentiles know not God and thus were excluded (I Thessalonians 4:5).

Most people do not believe that the United States is Israel; however, the United States is Israel (Hosea 1:10–11).

After the apostles contacted the Israelites, the Israelites returned to God's commandments. They were inspired to get away from their captors, the Assyrians, so they started to migrate away from the Caspian Sea area to the north and west into northern Europe and western Europe. This they started to do even before the apostles contacted them. Some groups traveled through North Africa, then to Spain until the Moors and the Italians took over the area; then on to the British Isles. Other groups went to southern Russia and eastern Europe, then moved on to Scandinavia, western Germany, northern Germany, France, Holland, Belgium, Luxembourg, Austria, Switzerland, Denmark, and the British Isles. Later on some moved on to the United States, Canada, Australia, and South Africa. Places that they traveled through were left with names identifying them. The tribe of Dan was especially noteworthy with regards to this, and they were apparently a front-runner and an aggressive group. The Danube River, Dniester River, Don River, Danapris River, Scandan(din)avia, the Danish nation, the city of Danbury, England, and the Danites who went from Spain to Ireland were all named from the tribe of Dan. The Saxons, the Angles (Anglo-Saxon), the Celts, the Normans, the Franks, the Britons, the Gaels, the Saxons, the Vikings, the Sacki, and the Saca are all Israelite peoples. Jacobs, Jacobsen, Jacoby, Isaac, and Isaacson are all Israelite names. These are all white people, descendants of Shem, Abraham, Isaac, and Jacob (Israel). (See exhibit 4.)

God commanded the Israelites not to intermarry with non-Israelites. The Israelites thus retained their "fair," meaning white, skin (Genesis 26:7) and, in many instances, blond hair. So wherever you find people who have a fair complexion and/or blond hair, you know that you are in an area where there are Israelites (I Samuel 17:42).

The United States, Canada, and Australia are splitoffs from the tribe of Joseph and are to receive, along with Great Britain, the inheritance granted to Joseph and then to his sons, Ephraim and Manasseh. Manasseh was to be a single great nation (the United States), and Ephraim was to be a greater company of nations (Great Britain, Canada, and Australia). There is no doubt that the people who immigrated into the United States and formed the thirteen colonies were Israelites from the tribe of Manasseh (Genesis 48:17–20).

Those early settlers in the United States from Europe knew of their heritage and followed the principles of the Bible. Because they did, the United States prospered and expanded (Deuteronomy 7:11–26). Some modern-day media types and Sunday-go-to-meeting types complain that the inhabitants of the lands at the time—Indians, Eskimos, and Spanish—were mistreated. But they should understand this, that the conquest of the lands of the United States by the Israelites was in accordance with God's covenant with Abraham, Isaac, Jacob (Israel), Joseph, and their descendants. The Israelites are a special people and are a clannish people. The United States is Israel. After the Israelites came out of Egypt, they were commanded not to marry outside of their tribes or to have anything to do with other tribes, in order to keep their inheritance (Numbers 36:5–13; Leviticus 18:1–5).

Almost the entire New Testament of the Bible was written to and for the United States and Great Britain, which are Israel. Most of the Old Testament is for the United States and Great Britain. The covenant given to Ephraim and Manasseh was not given to the other ten (or eleven, as it were) tribes of Israel. That is why it was important that the Israelites of the United States and Great Britain not marry people from any Gentile or heathen tribes.

There is a duality all through the Bible and the prophecies made to and for the old Israelites in the times of Abraham, Isaac, Jacob (changed to Israel), Joseph, David, Jeremiah, and others are also meaningful and in force for the descendants of those people in our times—now.

Chapter II

The Rise of the United States

To understand the inheritance of the United States you must go back to Genesis 48 in the Bible. Jacob, whose name was later changed to Israel, with God's blessing conferred on Manasseh the blessing of greatness. This blessing was that the descendants of Manasseh would become a great nation. Jacob also gave Ephraim a blessing of greatness in that the descendants would become a great multitude of nations. The greatest single and number-one nation of all time is the United States (Genesis 27:29). The greatest multitude of nations of all time was the British Empire. Thus the United States is the tribe of Manasseh, and Great Britain is the tribe of Ephraim. They are brother nations. The only thing that could change this blessing was if those people turned away from God's commandments and consorted with heathen and Gentile peoples and their activities. That is happening at the time of the end.

The early immigrants to the United States were from England. They settled along the east coast and formed the thirteen original colonies. The most noteworthy group were the Puritans, who rebelled against the ornaments and ceremonies retained in Britain's churches from Roman Catholic services. These Puritans established themselves in Massachusetts, Connecticut, and Rhode Island. These people and others from France and Germany wanted to escape persecution, harassment, and discrimination.

These people were banned from holding public office in their old countries. These were the people who firmly believed in the tenets of the Bible and followed biblical precepts in their lives, just like God commanded the Israelites to do. These people were Israelites.

Later on, the Dutch established themselves in New York and part of New Jersey near Philadelphia. This lasted forty years, or until the English took over their territory in 1664. These people were all Israelites.

People from Sweden established a settlement in Delaware, which was later taken over by the Dutch. Those people were all Israelites.

Settlers from England established themselves in Maryland, Virginia, New Hampshire, Maine, the Carolinas, and New Jersey. William Penn established Philadelphia and Pennsylvania with Germans, who were Pietists, with religious views similar to those of the Quakers. Later on James Oglethorpe established Georgia with people from England. Those people were all Israelites. Those people all came from the reservoir of people who had migrated to western Europe from the Caucasian Mountains area. They were heirs of the Christian religion and of its Scriptures, which taught the worth of the individual man, as opposed to the Catholic Church, which disseminated the idea that all people are spiritual beings potentially equal in the sight of God.

The voyage of John Cabot in 1497 to Nova Scotia and Newfoundland had invested the English sovereign with a title to the land of all North America with the right to govern his subjects residing there. Thus for a colony to start in America, it was necessary that they obtain the approval of the king of England. This the king gave by granting a royal charter or patent to the colonizers. Groups settling in the thirteen colonies were granted charters, or grants of land, by the king of England during the 1600s. The last of the thirteen colonies, Georgia, was given a charter in 1732.

Spain had acquired an empire in Central and South America by 1570, which brought on a conflict between Britain and Spain in which Britain came out on top. Britain then encouraged more settlement of colonies in America.

France had developed an interest in America with exploration and some settlements. There was much conflict between Britain and France over territorial rights in America. By the Treaty of Paris in 1763, Britain acquired Canada and other lands in North America westward to the Mississippi River, except for New Orleans.

Then there developed disagreements between the colonies and Britain over taxes and trade, which resulted in the Revolutionary War of 1775–83. When this ended it resulted in a formal peace treaty signed September 3, 1783, in Paris, in which the independence of the United States was recognized. As of that date all the thirteen colonies in America were Israel. The United States was an Israelite nation, of the tribe of Manasseh.

There was very little immigration during the 1700s and early 1800s. New births by the Israelites in the colonies provided additional population for expansion. After the Revolution and the establishment of government in the United States, settlers moved westward across the Appalachian Mountains and settled the territory to the Mississippi River. These were all Israelites.

By the Treaty of Paris in 1783, Britain transferred its claim to the Northwest Territory (Ohio, Indiana, Illinois, Michigan, and Wisconsin) from the Ohio River to the Canadian border to the United States. There was much conflict in this area with the Indians, but by the Treaty of

Greenville in 1795 the Indians accepted the white settlements. After 1830, many settlers came pouring in from Ireland, Scotland (Scotch-Irish), Germany, Wales, France, and Scandinavia. Those were all Israelites. They moved into the good farmland areas of the Midwest.

Then later, after the cities were built up and manufacturing establishments were built, many settlers came in from southern Europe, Russia, Poland, Hungary, and Czechoslovakia. These settlers were not Israelites. Most of these later settlers were Gentiles.

In the South, in 1798, the U.S. Congress created the Mississippi Territory covering all lands between Georgia and the Mississippi River. The area was expanded in 1804 to include the area north to Tennessee. Then in 1812, it was further expanded to include West Florida. The early settlers were English, French, Scotch-Irish, and northern European, all Israelites.

By the Treaty of Paris in 1783, in which Britain transferred its territorial claims to the United States, West Florida could not be transferred, because of a dispute with Spain. The dispute over West Florida was settled with Spain in 1798. After that was settled, West Florida then belonged to the United States.

North Carolina had claimed the territory called Tennessee Territory below the Ohio River. In 1789, North Carolina ceded its westward claim to the Tennessee Territory, to the United States. In 1790, Congress organized the whole Tennessee Territory into the Territory of the United States south of the Ohio River, and it was known as the Southwest Territory. The early settlers were English, Scotch, Irish, German, Dutch, and French. Those were all Israelites.

You will note that those people moving into the great farmland areas of the United States were Israelites. It was only later, after the cities were formed and the factories were built, that settlers from the non-Israelite areas of Europe began moving in. These people were from eastern and southern Europe and were mostly Gentiles. Also, the southern farmers began bringing in heathen people from Africa to work on the farms.

The biggest accumulation of territory by the United States was the Louisiana Purchase in 1803, when the United States acquired 800,000 square miles from France. This determined the westward orientation of the United States and was the basis for the United States to be a world power. James Monroe, as a minister to France appointed by Pres. Thomas Jefferson, negotiated the terms of the settlement. A treaty dated April 30, 1803, provided for the payment of $11,250,000 to France plus assumption of claims against France by U.S. citizens amounting to $3,750,000. By the Rush-Bagot Agreement of 1818 with Britain, Britain and the United States established the forty-ninth parallel from Lake of the Woods to the Rocky Mountains as the northern border of the Louisiana Purchase. This sale resulted from Napoléon's problems with Spain, especially concerning New Orleans and his impending war with Britain. Napoléon decided to sell the Louisiana Territory to finance that war. Also, aggressive American settlers who had moved into the area helped decide the sale. This purchase included New Orleans, which had been a problem for France.

By the Transcontinental Treaty of 1819, Spain ceded Florida to the United States at no cost. The United States did assume liability of up to $5 million in damages that Americans in Florida claimed against Spain. This resulted because Spain failed to govern Florida and apparently was not willing or able to fight the United States for the territory. Also, this resulted from the aggressive Americans moving into the area, and it was a haven for runaway slaves.

Settlers from the eastern states moved into Texas, which Mexico considered its territory because of Spanish settlements. There were many conflicts between Americans and Mexicans, and after a decisive victory at San Jacinto in 1836, the independence of Texas became an established fact. The Mexican government, however, did not recognize the republic of Texas. There were many problems in Texas, including financing. As a consequence, annexation by the United States was made in 1845. This resulted in a war between Mexico and the United States. By the Treaty of Guadalupe Hidalgo, the war between the United States and Mexico was ended. This treaty was ratified in 1848 and ceded the territories that now cover Texas, California, Nevada, Utah, most of Arizona and New Mexico, plus a portion of Oklahoma and Colorado to the United States. The United States paid Mexico $15 million and assumed $3,250,000 in claims by U.S. citizens against Mexico. In spite of the date of settlement of that war, Texas was actually annexed to the United States in 1845, resulting from aggressive Americans moving into and settling in the territory. These aggressive Americans were Israelites. The disputes with Mexico over the territory were settled by the war.

The Gadsden Purchase, a territory of 29,670 square miles, was acquired from Mexico in 1854, during Franklin Pierce's administration. It formed the southern parts of New Mexico and Arizona. The purchase price was $10 million. This purchase came about because of the turmoil resulting from the Treaty of Hidalgo. It settled a boundary dispute.

Britain and the United States had a joint interest in Oregon, Idaho, and Washington territory for several years. Many settlers moved in from the eastern United States and Canada. These lands were settled by farmers who were Israelites. On June 15, 1846, the Oregon Treaty was signed, which extended the international boundary along the forty-ninth parallel to the Juan de Fuca Strait, and thus this territory became part of the United States.

The United States obtained an interest in Alaska and some islands, but these are unimportant and immaterial to the rise of the United States as the nation of Israel. Alaska and Hawaii became states, but these acquisitions came after the decline of the United States began. The natives of Hawaii and Alaska are descendants from Japheth, the brown people, and thus are not Israelites. Because they are not Israelites, these areas should not have been annexed, unless the United States would have been willing to go in and destroy all the inhabitants and their works and convert the areas to an Israelite state.

The United States, as an Israelite nation, will prosper as long as it follows God's commandments (Leviticus 20:22–24). The prophecies of the Bible pertain mostly to the United States and Great Britain, for they are the tribes of Manasseh and Ephraim, whose father was Joseph and who are Israel. This was because of a special covenant from God given to Jacob, changed to Israel, their grandfather (Deuteronomy 10:12–13, 22, 11:8–12). Every place that the people of Israel cared to go, God would give the land to them and drive out the inhabitants (Deuteronomy 12:1–5, 29–32).

The blessings of the United States and its people, if they follow the Ten Commandments, which the United States did in the 1700s and 1800s and until 1950, are listed in Deuteronomy 28:1–14. After World War II, the people of the United States started doing abominable things, more and more, until today the United States is a cesspool of evil, and as a consequence, Deuteronomy 28:15–68 tells what will happen to the United States. See also the Book of Ezekiel. It was written for Israel.

The downfall of Great Britain has already preceded that of the United States. The British were at one time the greatest power on the earth. Now Britain is about a second-rate power. It cannot defend the Falkland Islands without help from outside. It has gone to the European Common Market, begging with hand out, as it were, to survive. What has happened first in Britain will happen later on in the United States, because Great Britain and the United States are brothers and are mirrors of each other. Things will happen first in Great Britain; then a short time later the same things will happen in the United States.

Many people think that the words of the Old Testament of the Bible do not pertain to our times. Some think that Jesus did away with those things. That is not true. The prophets of olden times spoke with authority from God, and it was for all times (Deuteronomy 29:29). The only things that Jesus did away with were the animal sacrifices and circumcision. The Bible has a duality all the way through it. Prophecies and things that happened in early times are also for the end-times and thus duplicated. That is one of the keys to understanding. For instance, in just one example, there was an exodus of the Israelites from captivity in Egypt and also at the end-time there is and will be an exodus of Israelites from their captivity to the promised land, Jerusalem.

Recently there has been criticism by some misinformed people of the actions by the Israelites of the United States toward other peoples originally in the area of the United States, such as Indians, Eskimos, and the Spanish.

The criticism is entirely unjustified. Please refer to Deuteronomy 7:1–6 and 7:16–26. The United States is Israel, and the land was chosen by God (II Samuel 7:10; Numbers 33:50–56) for the Israelites' home.

This chapter covers how the United States, a nation of Israelites, became the greatest single nation of all time. There are twenty-four events leading to the decline and captivity of the United States. The decline of the United States and the reasons therefore are covered in the following chapters.

Chapter III
Breakdown of the Homes

The first thing that occurred to result in the destruction of the United States was the breakdown of the home environment. The home is the safe haven where members of the family assemble when they are done with the affairs of the day. It is the place where family values are developed through reading, playing, discussion, and discipline.

The breakdown occurred because of many things. Because of the labor-saving gadgets that were invented or developed, there is much more leisure time; because of the satanic TV and radio programs, because of the educational system that has gone haywire, because of affluence, and because of the lust for money, power, and pleasures, the people have no time for family anymore, but only for personal pleasures to satisfy their egos.

The beginning of the breakdown of the home environment was the granting of the right to vote to women back in 1920. The Bible says that when a man and woman get married they become one—not two, but one unit. God is the head of the church, the church is the head of man, and man is head of his wife and family (Ephesians 5:22–25; I Corinthians 11:3). Wives are to be in subjection to their husbands (Genesis 3:16; I Peter 3:1–6; Colossians 3:18–19; Romans 7:2–3). In a home unit, the man and wife are to discuss the affairs pertaining to them and their family, and then the head of the household, the man, makes the decision. When women got the right to vote, they began lusting for power and then began telling their husbands to buzz off. The Bible guidance is I Corinthians 14:34–35, which says that a woman is not to speak in a church, but to ask of her husband (Numbers 30:6–16; Mark 10:8).

Another event causing great destruction of the home was the passage of the Civil Rights Bill in 1964 and the antidiscrimination laws by Congress. With the Civil Rights Bill women could leave their homes and go out into the world, with equal rights in hiring, get jobs formerly held by men, dress like men, smoke and drink like men, and indulge in many other things like men, all with the blessing of a Congress that they had elected in order to get their desires. The Bible is pretty clear as to the roles of men and women in society. The Bible also says that it is an abomination for a women to wear men's clothing, just like it is an abomination for a man to dress up in women's clothes (Deuteronomy 22:5).

Another development that facilitated the breakdown of the homes, is the proliferation of birth control information and devices. With this information, women can now go out in society and also in their own homes act like the whore. This also gives them more time to indulge in pursuits that please their lustful fantasies but are an abomination.

Congress and state legislative bodies have granted all kinds of tax writeoffs and credits for women who have turned the guidance and upbringing of their children over to strangers in day-care centers and schools, even to the extent of feeding the children breakfast and lunch. The Bible insists that parents must raise their children up to be sober, well mannered, without fault, adults in the manner of good society and tenets of the Bible (Titus 1:6, Titus 2). God holds the parents responsible for this, not someone outside the family (Proverbs 22:6). It always astonished me as to how parents could think of turning their children over to anyone else to supervise. A parent who does not control his son shall die (Ezekiel 18:10–13).

Another serious development in the breakdown of the homes is the granting of legal separations and divorce. Divorce is wrong except in cases of adultery, in which case neither party should marry or have any sexual relations with anyone else. That would be adultery also. Some Israelites in the United States are marrying heathen and Gentiles. This is an abomination (Exodus 34:16; Nehemiah 10:30; II Corinthians 6:14–17). Israelites should not even associate with heathen (I Corinthians 5:9–13; II Thessalonians 3:14). Anyone who does is in danger of losing his God-decreed inheritance. An Israelite must not marry anyone who is not an Israelite (Genesis 24:3–4). A house divided against itself is headed for destruction and desolation (Luke 11:17). Because Israelites are marrying non-Israelites, that is undoubtedly a factor in the high divorce rate. A lot of people have lost track of their true identity. People should give very serious thought to marriage before going into it.

With the building of apartment complexes and condominiums people are jammed up next to each other, without space to conduct their home life in accordance with the Bible. Along with that, the antidiscrimination laws concerning housing are an abomination. Society and government laws, rules, and regulations are to blame for those things. As a consequence it is difficult for a family to run their household like God wants them to run it (Isaiah 5:8–9).

The responsibility for the Christian character of a home is on the shoulders of the man. A man must provide for his family. Those that do not are worse than an infidel

(I Timothy 5:8). Those who abandon their family are also wrong and in real trouble.

Parents are bowing to the wishes of their children and are voting into office those people favoring the wants of children. The legislatures are outlawing spanking, which God says should be done to correct bad behavior (Hebrews 12:5–10; Proverbs 13:24, 23:13). Because the parents have abdicated their responsibility, the children are ruling the homes, with the advice and consent of the mother. They seem to be able to get anything they want from their parents. Without proper supervision children are committing all kinds of bad things—vandalism, drinking, drug activities, whoredoms, satanism, and whatever else they can think of to do. Children are the oppressors, ruling with the advice and consent of women (Isaiah 3:12). The father has forgotten the fact that he is the head of the household or else has become wimpish and abdicated. Many households are being destroyed and families broken up (Matthew 12:25; Proverbs 22:6, 15).

Children are to obey their parents in all things (Colossians 3:20–21). It is really sad that legislatures, the media, and the welfare agency personnel think that they know better how your child should be raised. They are in for the shock of their lives someday. A rebellious son shall be killed (Deuteronomy 21:18–21). Most legislatures, welfare agencies, and the media want to coddle children and furnish them with expensive counseling, which in most cases appears to do no good and is wrong in the first place (Ezekiel 18:10–13). Those that curse their father or mother shall die (Leviticus 20:9). God says that he changes not, and the commandments and tenets of the Bible are in effect today as well as olden times (Malachi 3:6).

As an aside, servants and also hired help in factories and businesses are to obey their employer (Colossians

3:22). This brings into question some of the labor union policies and practices.

Congress, and state legislative bodies which make the laws resulting in many of the abominations listed above, and the judges who compound the abominations are a stench in the nostrils of God. God condemns lawyers (Luke 11:45–52), but they are only doing, in most cases, the will of the majority of the people.

Chapter IV

Women Taking Over Management and Administrative Positions

A second event causing the destruction of the United States is the astounding development of women forcing themselves into positions of management in government, business, and industry. This is contrary to the tenets of the Bible. Man has always been the designated head of any organization, starting with the home (I Corinthians 11:3; Genesis 3:16).

In the United States no woman has gotten into the position of head of state or president. They are working on it and may obtain it before long. You will note that in every instance where a woman was placed at the head of any government, that country immediately deteriorated, some cases to a state bordering on anarchy. Look at what happened to Argentina, India, Pakistan, the Philippines, Great Britain, and the Netherlands. While Argentina and India now have men at the head of government, the breakdown and disorder that occurred during the time that a woman was the head of government continues on to some extent today. Pakistan and the Philippines are supported by the taxpayers of the United States as sort of welfare cases. Argentina is bankrupt and much killing has gone on there. The killing and disorder in India are as bad. The Netherlands was once a world power but has lost all its colonies and is noted for its prostitution. Great Britain, which was once the world's greatest power, is now a second-rate power, having lost almost all of its colonies. It can't even defend the Falklands without help from the United States.

If the United States ever elects a woman president, the same thing that happened to Great Britain will happen to the United States. The same thing will happen to the United States if the United States ever elects a president who is not from an Israelite tribe. All presidents of the United States to date have had a background genealogy in one of the tribes of Israel. God will not permit a non-Israelite to rule for long a nation of Israel, nor, for that matter, anyone whom God does not approve.

Women are deserting their homes, putting on men's clothes, and putting themselves, by means of affirmative action law, into management, administrative, professional, and almost every other work position that men should be doing in accordance with the tenets of the Bible. The Bible spells out the roles of men and women (Colossians 3:18–19; I Timothy 2:9–15). Women are going to exercise classes to make themselves slim and trim. This is contrary to the tenets of the Bible (I Timothy 4:8). Women are taking up smoking and drinking, presumably to present themselves as equal to men. It is an abomination for a woman to wear clothing pertaining to a man (Deuteronomy 22:5). A large percentage of women are dressing that way. Adornments are an abomination (Genesis 35:2–4).

Women are putting on jewelry, perfume, and other adornments to make themselves attractive to others, to promote themselves in business, politics, socially, or whatever, and it is wrong (I Peter 3:3; I Timothy 2:9–14). Nearly all of them do it. This will bring destruction to them (Isaiah 3:16–24).

At the end-time, women will live with men for convenience sake rather than for God's purpose (Isaiah 4:1). You see or hear about it all the time now (Proverbs 11:22). Women are changing their natural use to that which is against nature (Romans 1:25–32). Related to this also is the fact that women are becoming athletes, which is against nature. Lesbian relationships are an abomination.

The most revealing commandment of the Bible concerning women is in I Corinthians 14:34–35, in which it states that women in a church are not to speak but are to ask of their husbands.

There was an instance where a woman took over as a head of a nation and destruction and death came to her because of it (II Kings 11). Jezebel, who was a queen, did not follow God's commandments and was killed and eaten by dogs (II Kings 9:30–37). Some might refer to Deborah, said to be a prophetess in early times. But this was during a period of time when Israel was so evil that God had sent them into captivity by Canaan (Judges 4:1–5). Israel was not a nation at this time.

Women can be saved through childbearing, provided that they follow God's commandments and ordinances (I Timothy 2:15).

Women preachers and prophetesses are an abomination (Ezekiel 13:17–23).

Chapter V
Destroying the Careers of the Leaders

A third event causing the decline and captivity of the United States is the ridiculing of the leaders by the media, making fun of the leaders by the comics, and taking into court on frivolous charges those who are trying to do the best things for the United States according to God's will rather than men's will (James 4:11–12). One sees it more and more on TV, on radio, and in the newspapers. What the leaders say and do is picked apart and many times made fun of. They are not given a chance to lead. You hear it said many times now that a good administrator or executive would not want to run for public office or accept a government appointment, because it would subject him to harassment and criticism. Besides, most good executives can make more money in the private sector. Thus the United States does not have the best people running the country.

In olden times, when Israel was growing, those who questioned the actions of the leaders were put to death without trial (Joshua 1:18). God controls the affairs of Israel. In an Israelite nation, and the United States is Israel, God himself would not allow anyone to be a leader, for long, who did not follow his will (Leviticus 10:1–2; Deuteronomy 17:14–15).

In an Israelite nation, God allows good men to be put into leadership positions, and if God feels that his plan is not being carried out, then the leadership is taken away (Deuteronomy 1:8–15). God would not permit the assassination of a king or president to take place unless he felt that his plan for the earth was not being carried out (I Samuel 2:6). Men that rule must be just, ruling with the fear of God (II Samuel 23:3; Deuteronomy 1:16–17). Rulers are to be obeyed (Titus 3:1–2; Hebrews 13:17; Ecclesiastes 8:1–4). God, not man, will hold accountable any leader who fails. Great men are not always wise (Job 32:9), but people should respect them (I Timothy 2:1–3). God makes and breaks rulers and administrators, destroying those quickly who depart from God's plan for earth (Job 34:21–30, 36:6–12). He hears and sees all that goes on around the earth (Proverbs 8:15–16).

There is a lack of respect for the elders in the United States in today's times, and it is increasing more and more. Young men shall be silent, and old men shall stand up in the presence of greatness (Job 29:7–10). Because the schools are teaching students to do their thing, whatever seems good, the people are becoming disrespectful of old, established rules and regulations. If one sees or hears of things that he thinks are wrong, there are peaceful ways to express other opinions. In a democratic society and a Christian society, it is completely wrong to disrupt the affairs of the world by violent demonstrations, sit-ins, or other disruptions (Exodus 23:2). Any demonstrator who destroys property, hurts another person, or hurts a business will answer to God. It is wickedness (Ecclesiastes 5:8).

While the leaders are to be obeyed and are to have respect (Hebrews 13:17), flattering titles shall not be given to any person (Job 32:21–22). Rich men will be destroyed (Job 27:19–23; Matthew 19:24; Mark 10:25; James 5:1–5), because rich men have a tendency to spend their money on foolish things. If a rich man lets his money be used for

Christian efforts, God will see that he gets more riches. Christian efforts are not necessarily those that the Sunday churches or the media promote, but what God says is good as stated in the Bible.

Anyone who attempts to harm or destroy the person or character of one of God's chosen people will suffer a quick death (I Peter 3:12–13). Situations concerning this are well known.

Chapter VI
Breakdown of Morals

A fourth reason and probably the most important causing the United States to decline and to go into captivity is the breakdown of morals in the United States (II Timothy 3:1–6). The Ten Commandments of the Bible are the guide for proper living and relationships with others for Israelites and those who desire to become part of an Israelite nation (Romans 7:1). Very few people seem to follow them anymore (Deuteronomy 27:15–26; Exodus 20). Guidelines for Christian living are stated in Exodus 22, Exodus 23, Leviticus 19:11–37, Colossians 3:5–6, and Galatians 5:19–21.

In addition to the Ten Commandments, which were reinforced by Jesus (Romans 13:8–10), another commandment was added by Jesus—that you "love one another" (John 13:34). Love is not lust, but a desire to please your neighbor (I John 4:7–21, 5:2–3; James 1:14–15), provided that person is a Christian person. A common attitude today is to treat everyone as a brother. That is not so. God commands God's people not to associate with those that are disorderly, that is, those that drink excessively, indulge in drugs, indulge in fornication or adultery, and/or commit vandalism and lies (II Corinthians 6:14–15; II Thessalonians 3:6, 14). The people of the United States are more and more doing those things that are not proper to do. The most important of those things are covered in this chapter.

Teaching the right things to the children is the responsibility of both parents. People seem to have forgotten that the father is the head of the household and that the mother is the homemaker, teacher, and guide for her children, because she is with them most of the time (I Corinthians 11:1–15). God commands parents that when they have children, they must bring them up right with God. There is no justification for divorce except in some cases of adultery. If there should be divorce, then neither party should marry again. Living together without marriage is wrong because you are thumbing your nose at God and society. While sex itself is sin (Romans 7:5), marriage procedures were put into effect to provide for a record of lifetime commitments under biblical precepts and to prevent innocent people from being trapped into adultery or fornication and thus being condemned by God (I Corinthians 6:9; Numbers 5:20–27; Luke 16:18; Romans 6:13).

Homosexuality is an abomination (Leviticus 18:22, 20:13; Romans 1:24–32). Sodom and Gomorrah were destroyed because of their wrong sex practices. Homosexuals will be killed. There is an unfair attitude by some people in these later days in that some consider all single adults as being homosexuals. That attitude is wrong. God's people are given power to do what is right and power to not do what is wrong. It is possible for a single person to live a morally right life (Revelation 14:1–5; Luke 20:35).

Another reason for the breakdown of morals is the fact that mothers are not staying home and teaching their children the right things. So many mothers are out working in some office or factory, and the guidance of their children is left to some stranger in a day-care center. That is completely wrong. God says that parents are responsible for the upbringing of their children (Proverbs 22:6). No parent can enter into God's Kingdom unless he follows the Ten Commandments and sees that his children are raised as Christians to be sober, moral, honorable, and trustworthy individuals (Titus 1:6, 2:12; I Peter 2:9) Any mother or father who has a child that does not have a Christian character is in serious trouble with God (II John; I Timothy 2:15; Matthew 3:8–10; Luke 3:8–9). If a person cannot rule his home, how can he be trusted to rule in God's Kingdom (Proverbs 23:13)?

Another factor in the breakdown of morals is that the schools of the United States are teaching children that whatever seems right for them is right. That is wrong. That is the way of Satan. The schools of the United States are Satan's workshops. The emphasis in schools now is on sports rather than on learning. The schools of the United States have about as many teachers teaching sports as they have those teaching other things. Sports now means competition to outdo or outperform the other person or team. Winning at all costs is the focus in our schools, colleges, and universities. That is Satan's handiwork. Instead of learning reading, writing, history, geography, and social sciences, the students are learning how to beat another person in a game. It is no wonder that the students of the United States cannot read, write, or speak intelligently when they are *allowed* to graduate. Teaching things such as discipline, the rights of other people, and how to get along with other people seems to be lacking in the schools of the United States.

Another factor in the breakdown of morals is the media—the TV shows, including talk shows, the picture shows, and the radio music. There is much violence, sex, and loud and bad language in those, which are an abomination. Some churches recognize the problem and are advising the members to get rid of their TVs or at least turn them off. But not enough are doing that. Everyone should turn off their TVs until they change their programming, boycott the motion picture houses, and turn off their radios when satanic or suggestive talk or music comes on. It seems that the whole reason for TV is lust for money and pleasure. Occasionally there is a good, worthwhile program, but it is a rare occurrence. The TV programs as well as the schools of the United States promote "do your own thing," "win at all costs," and "get an advantage over the next person." Winning or getting ahead of the next person is the main program being presented. Conning the other person is looked on as sharp or smart in today's society.

Sexual relations with more than one person is fornication in case of an unmarried person and adultery in the case of a married person and is condemned (I Thessalonians 4:2–7, 6:9; Leviticus 19:29; I Peter 2:11). It is destruction (I Thessalonians 4:2–5). It makes a whore or whoremonger out of a person (Mark 10:11–12; Jeremiah 3:1–3). The only exception to sexual relations with more than one person is in the case of a widow, who may remarry (I Timothy 5:11–14; I Corinthians 7:8–9), except she cannot marry a priest (Leviticus 21:14; Ezekiel 44:22). Adulterers and rapists shall be killed (II Samuel 13; Deuteronomy 22:13–30). No bastard or mongrel, which is the proper interpretation, shall enter into God's church (Deuteronomy 23:1–2). A mongrel is the offspring of an Israelite and a non-Israelite, regardless of whether the parents are married or not married. Those Israelites who go after strange flesh will suffer the fate of Sodom and Gomorrah (Jude 7). There shall be no whore in an Israelite nation, nor any sodomy (Deuteronomy 23:17). Sodomites as well as idols are to be removed from an Israelite nation (I Kings 15:12). If adultery, fornication, and sodomy are permitted, they will increase until a whole nation is polluted and destroyed (James 1:14–15), as had been happening to the United States. At the end-time, people will lose their sense of common decency (Deuteronomy 28:30–32, 53–59).

Those people who steal, those who get drunk on liquor or high on drugs, those who use abusive or contemptuous language toward another person, those who covet another person's wife or property, and those who hold a person for ransom to extort money, property, or favors shall not come into God's Kingdom (I Corinthians 6:10). The United States is one of the worst places in the world where those activities are carried on. The uninformed or wimpish authorities provide millions of dollars to accommodate, counsel, and try to rehabilitate people who do such things (Proverbs 17:15). It is wrong. Delinquents are inhabited by devils (Mark 1:32).

One of the most erroneous promotions now, which shows the ignorance of the promoters, is that alcoholism is a disease. The Bible says that no drunkard can enter into God's Kingdom (I Corinthians 6:10). A person who takes a drink of alcohol beverage does so of his own free will. Each person is responsible for his own actions. Drinking is a morals problem, pure and simple. Methinks that those who try to promote alcoholism as a disease are in the promotion business to drum up careers for themselves.

Satan, a spirit being, can enter into the body of an individual and make that individual do evil things (Luke 22:3).

If two people marry and they have children, then they must see that their children are raised in a Christian manner (Ezekiel 18:10–17). A single person can live a Christian life (I Corinthians 7:1; Luke 20:35; Proverbs 21:9; Revelation 14:1–5). Gay men and lesbians are condemned (Romans 1:18–32).

People who worship or have as an idol any object such as a statue, sun, moon, star, totem pole, mystic, TV star, motion picture star, singer, sports figure, sports car, animal, etc., cannot enter into God's Kingdom (Ephesians 5:5; Deuteronomy 16:22, 17:2–5). That is idolatry. When people have much money to spend, many search out weird, unusual, and dangerous ways to spend it, ways that titillate them but are contrary to the tenets of the Bible. People like to boast of what they have or what they can do—to show off—but it is nothing but vanity (Ecclesiastes 2:1–16). Millions of people indulge in those activities (Luke 16:15).

Men who wear women's clothes and women who wear men's clothes cannot enter in God's Kingdom (Deuteronomy 22:5). Women especially are now dressing like men, and this is an abomination. People who indulge in violence, such as a boxer or a football player, cannot enter into God's Kingdom.

The welfare system in the United States is wrong, God commands that those who will not work shall not eat (II Thessalonians 3:10). One of the consequences of the liberal welfare system in the United States is that the poor, lame, and lazy of the world are coming to the United States for welfare handouts.

God commands that a person should not accept a gift where a favor is expected (Exodus 23:8). The gifts and also the political contributions–they are gifts—amount to billions of dollars each year (Deuteronomy 16:19).

Any person who kills another person, unless it is an accident, shall be put to death (Exodus 21:12–15; Numbers 35:16–31; Leviticus 24:17–22). The authorities in the United States spend millions of dollars trying to rehabilitate those individuals who commit murder when the answer to the situation has always been in the Bible. If an animal kills a person and the owner of the animal knew it was a mean animal, then the owner of the animal shall be put to death (Exodus 21:29).

Nakedness if forbidden, even between relatives (Leviticus 18:6–19), except for a husband and wife. Nakedness itself was not sin. What God made is perfect, and a person should not be ashamed of what is perfect. But when Adam and Eve sinned, then nakedness became an embarrassment to mankind. When it became an embarrassment to mankind, then it became sin (Genesis 3:5–7).

A false witness shall be punished (Deuteronomy 19:16–21). It seems more and more that there are doubts about truthfulness of testimony in the courts of the United States and truthfulness of information entered on application forms of various types. In the early days of the United States, when the court system was set up by Christians for Christians who understood the tenets of the Bible, the court system worked well. Now, when so many heathen and others who don't follow Christ or the Bible are being involved in court proceedings, the courts' decisions are very questionable and one wonders whether the truth is getting out.

A rebellious son shall be put to death (Deuteronomy 21:18–21). It seems that in the United States it is the policy to coddle them and furnish them expensive counseling at taxpayers' expense, which is wrong (Ezekiel 18:10–13).

A person is not to consult an astrologer for counsel. King Saul died because he consulted an astrologer rather than God (I Samuel 28:7–25, 31:3–6). There is much activity of this type in the United States now, and it is wrong. Witches, sorcerers, wizards, and dealers in familiar spirits are condemned (Leviticus 20:27). No diviner, witch, consulter of familiar spirits, or astrologers shall be allowed in an Israelite nation (Deuteronomy 18:10–12; II Kings 21:6–7; Exodus 22:18).

It is a sin to have a census in a nation of Israel (I Chronicles 21:1–17). Each ten years, the United States makes a grand to-do about counting all the people in the United States, and it is wrong. Also, look at the numerous polls taken of how people are thinking. It is the same thing. The whole purpose of a census or poll is for certain groups to get an advantage over other people.

God commands that Israelites are not to buy or sell on the Sabbath Day, which is the seventh day of the week (Isaiah 56:2; Exodus 20:10). Jesus observed the seventh day of the week as the Sabbath Day. No work is to be done on the Sabbath Day. In the United States the seventh day, Saturday, is the biggest day of the week regarding sales and sporting activities. Even by just this you can see what God thinks of the United States (Nehemiah 10:31).

A person who gets drunk is in serious trouble with God (Isaiah 5:11). The same can be said of drug users. Here again, the authorities in the United States want to spend millions of taxpayer dollars to coddle drug users and give them counseling. A Christian should be in complete control of his mind and actions at all times. It cannot be otherwise.

Christmas trees, as well as the whole Christmas scene, are wrong (Jeremiah 10:1–5). Yet in the United States Christmas is the biggest event of the year. Halloween and Valentine's Day are also wrong. They are all pagan customs. People who follow pagan customs are condemned (Ezekiel 36:6–7; Psalms 59:8, 79:6–7).

People must not deal in blood (Acts 21:25). The blood of a human is the lifeblood for that person alone. Transfusions and storing blood on shelves are wrong; eating, cooking, and drinking animal blood are wrong (Leviticus

17:10). Yet the medical profession is superseding the will of God and playing God when they perform transfusions. With all the sicknesses resulting from transfusions, it shows how wrong they are (Acts 15:20, 20:26; Leviticus 3:17, 7:26–27; Psalms 72:14; Isaiah 59:3; Ezekiel 33:6, 8; Genesis 9:3–6).

No usury can be charged against another Israelite; however, on one who is not an Israelite it is permitted (Deuteronomy 23:19–20). The United States is doing just the opposite. The banks are lending money to Gentile and heathen countries at very little interest, and those countries are not paying the interest. In many cases, they are not even paying the loan back. The banks and lending institutions are charging the citizens of the United States up to 20 percent interest, which is usury. An Israelite nation may lend but must not borrow (Deuteronomy 15:6). Look at what the United States is doing with regard to that. It is just the opposite. An individual Israelite could lend to another Israelite who is in need (Deuteronomy 15:7–14). Every seven years debts will be canceled between Israelites, but not with a foreigner or stranger—a non-Israelite (Deuteronomy 15:1–3; Nehemiah 10:31).

The punishment for the sins of the parents is passed down to the fourth generation (Exodus 34:7). With all the defective children being born to sinful parents, there soon won't be enough whole and healthy people to take care of the defective ones or money to pay for their keep.

Marriage is honorable (John 2:1–9), provided it is not profaned (Hebrews 13:4; Luke 20:34–36). God commands that Israelites not marry outside of their tribes; otherwise they lose their inheritance, such as health, prosperity, and safety (Numbers 36; Nehemiah 10:30; Joshua 23:11–13; Deuteronomy 7:3; Jude 7). You see much intermarriage today in the United States. It is an abomination, and Israelites shall perish off the land. This means that a member of the tribe of Manasseh (United States) should not marry anyone who is not of the tribe of Manasseh and must not marry someone who is not an Israelite (Nehemiah 13:27). However, the elect (the 144,000) will not marry (Luke 20:35–36; Revelation 14:1–5).

Over the years in the United States, probably the greatest influence regarding the breakdown of morals has been that of the motion picture industry and the TV industry, and it is getting worse every year. Their purpose seems to be to make people laugh and feel good. To get people hyped up, they resort to canned laughter. Making their programs ridiculous and weird programs seems to be standard procedure in the entertainment industry. Then fools think that that is the way normal life is to be. The result is more and more deviation away from God's word (Ecclesiastes 7:3–6; Luke 20:34–36).

There is a proliferation of counseling and psychiatry. The schools are turning out thousands of counselors who earn huge salaries. People are urged to get counseling or psychiatric help for every problem, even little problems. They are condemning themselves (Isaiah 30:1). The answer to every problem and every question is in the Bible, for free (Isaiah 30:8–13). I have often said that our Sunday preachers are substitute psychiatrists—take your choice; go to a psychiatrist and pay him for soothing words or go to a Sunday church and hear soothing words from the preacher and pay your money into the collection plate.

Nowadays it seems that everyone wants to do his thing, brought about to a great extent by the superseding of parental authority by the schools and by government edicts and self-appointed authoritarian figures in government and in the media. Jesus gave the people the proper guidance and guidelines in Luke 6:20–49, and it also exists in the Ten Commandments.

An Israelite nation whose people do not obey the Ten Commandments will not win a war (Numbers 14:41–45). That is why the United States did not win the Vietnam War.

Those who live immorally or wickedly reap God's wrath (Job 4:8–9, 20:5–9), even those who prosper and get rich (Job 21:7–18). To those people that are good he gives wisdom (Ecclesiastes 2:26). "It is easier for a camel to go through the eye of a needle than for a rich man to enter into the Kingdom of God" (Luke 18:24–25; Matthew 19:24; Mark 10:25). No one ever saw a camel go through the eye of a needle (James 1:10–11). A rich man is more interested in his idols or pleasures than in God's word. Those who change their ways and follow God's word can be saved (Isaiah 55:7, 56:3–7). How? If God chooses to change them to spirit beings, then they can go through the eye of a needle (Matthew 19:25–26).

Those that do not believe God's word are accursed (Galatians 1:8–12). God's word does not please men, because it restricts them in what they think they would like to do. God hides the Gospel from those that do not believe in his word (II Corinthians 4:3–4). Many people of the United States have forgotten or perhaps were so wrapped up in worldly affairs that they never knew the guidelines for moral and Christian behavior outlined in Galatians 5:14–26, Exodus 20, Ephesians 5:5, Romans 12, and the Ten Commandments.

Some of the Sunday churches preach that when Jesus came the first time he did away with the Ten Commandments. That is not true (Romans 3:31, 6:1–2, 15, 23). The Ten Commandments are in force today (I John 2:3–4; Matthew 5:17–48, 19:16–19; Romans 13:9). Only those who keep the Ten Commandments can be saved (Romans 2:12–13). God commands a person not to love the affairs of the world, the lust of life, the pride of accomplishment (Romans 12:2; Galatians 1:4; I John 2:15–17). You hear the word "pride" spoken often, especially by athletes. Those that use it are condemning themselves.

Also, in addition to breaking God's laws, people are more and more breaking or ignoring the laws of the United States, laws that were established to provide for safe, sane, and moral communities. God says that all ordinances by man are to be obeyed (I Peter 2:13–14) unless they contradict any of God's laws.

The whole duty of man is to fear God and keep his commandments (Ecclesiastes 12:13–14). No one can be saved and obtain eternal life unless he follows the Ten Commandments (Luke 18:18–20; Hebrews 5:9). There can be no peace for the wicked (Isaiah 48:22). Evil will fall to anyone who does not follow the Ten Commandments (Jeremiah 6:19). Because people are inherently sinful, only with God's help can they overcome sin (Jeremiah 17:7–11). Each person is a temple of God, and no one should defile a temple of God by smoking, drinking to excess, using drugs, or cutting or abusing himself. God will hold a person accountable for doing any of those things (I Corinthians 3:16–17). The heathen and Gentiles know not God (I Thessalonians 4:5), but even the heathen and Gentiles can be saved by accepting Christ and following God's commandments, which everyone must follow in order to have eternal life (Deuteronomy 4:1–15, 5.1–21; Romans 2:6–8; I Corinthians 6:9–10; Galatians 3:28–29). The commandments are for all generations and for all times (Deuteronomy 7:9).

An aside as an example of the haywire thinking that goes on in the United States is the actions of the animal rights activists. Animals were put on earth for a purpose, some as aids and assistants for man to do his work, some to provide meat for man, some to provide clothing for man, some to provide meat for other animals, some as scavengers to clean the earth, and dogs as companions for man. Man is commanded to subdue the earth, including the animals, and to use them for whatever purpose is deemed necessary to accomplish the subduing of the earth. Animals are not like people, but some people seem to think that they should be treated just like people. The taking of animals out of their natural environment and placing them in zoos for people to ogle is an abomination. Animals should be left in their own natural environment. Dogs should not be chained or tied up. Dogs naturally like to romp around (Numbers 4:6; Acts 2:46; Proverbs 27:26; Exodus 12:3–4).

Many people think that it is wrong to put evildoers to death. I presume that they get this from the Sunday (modern) churches. Even for a simple thing such as cursing his father or mother one shall be put to death (Leviticus 20:9). Evildoers shall be put to death. Taxpayers' money should not be spent coddling them, furnishing them counseling, or furnishing them room and board and recreation facilities in an institution. The death should be quick. Chapter 20 of Leviticus gives many precepts for Christian living. Molech was a heathen god to whom children were sacrificed. This is completely condemned. Adulterers and fornicators shall be killed (Deuteronomy 22:13–30).

Probably the thing that God hates most, outside of worshiping other Gods and adultery and fornication, is lying. People don't seem to care much anymore whether they tell the truth. Even the government of the United States gets into the act of lying when they process documents that change the surnames of individuals. Surnames, such as Smith, Patterson, and thousands of others, have been passed down through the ages from generation to generation identifying a clan of people. Upstarts who adopt those surnames through government assistance are a big lie. The Bible says that no liar can enter into the Kingdom of God (I Timothy 1:10; Revelation 21:8).

People have adopted many little things as gods. Earrings are idols and thus gods (Genesis 35:2–4). Necklaces are the same. Statues are gods. All these things are an abomination and are to be put out of Israel (the United States).

So many things are backward in the society of the United States today. That is because Satan is the god of this world now for just a little more time. The Lord God is a God of war. God stirs up nations and peoples to make war so as to accomplish his purpose here on earth. Satan is a man of peace. That is why we have so many leaders of today proclaiming peace when there is no peace (Exodus 15:3). There can be no peace in the civilization of our times—not until Jesus returns to earth. God led the children of Israel out of Egypt on a roundabout way through the wilderness because he did not want them to see war with the Philistines at that time (Exodus 13:17). Later on the Israelites destroyed the people in that area.

God says that you shall not gather together to march as a protest, i.e., a protest march or a sit-in, to wrest judgment (Exodus 23:2). In the modern-day United States one sees many groups gathering together to try to get laws changed or companies or individuals to change their policies. Those protesters who gather together are on a one-way street to condemnation.

God says that you shall not tolerate or approve the poor in their cause—that is, to obtain free housing, free meals, free medical care, etc. (Exodus 23:3). A matter related to this is the United Way drives and other drives where people are coerced and even threatened in order to get them to contribute to a fund to help the poor. God does not approve helping evil people. God does approve helping one's Christian neighbors who are in difficulty, but only on a one-on-one basis, and in secret, I might add. When the names of people who give aid are published in the media or they are given certificates for humanitarian service, then their reward is of man and not of God. In other words, they have done it for puffing up their status in the community. That is condemnation in the eyes of God. (Matthew 6:1–4).

"Anyone who sacrificeth or pays tithes to any God but the Lord shall be destroyed" (Exodus 22:20). Does the church or person you give your money to teach God's word of the commandments and tenets of the Bible?

God puts wisdom into the hearts of *his* people to make good things and good decisions (Exodus 31:6). That is why practically all the chief inventions have been made by Israelites.

God redeems all the firstborn males of the Israelites (Exodus 13:12–16).

Summarizing, in the last days, people will be lovers of their own selves, covetous, boasters, proud, blasphemers, disobedient to parents, unthankful, unholy, without natural affection, trucebreakers, false accusers, incontinent, fierce, despisers of those that are good, traitors, heady, high-minded, lovers of pleasures more than lovers of God, having a form of godliness of self-righteousness, but denying God. That is exactly a description of the people of the United States today. You see it in the movies, on TV, especially in the sports events, in the churches, in the meeting halls, on the streets, in the business offices, in the factories, and everywhere. The main culprits in the degradation of society in the United States are the churches and the schools that promote "do your own thing" (II Timothy 3:1–7).

One of the most astonishing things that one hears is the statement by many that anything can be justified by the Bible. God does not change rules or change his mind (Malachi 3:6). His commandments and tenets are well established in the Bible. Commandments and rules that were in effect in olden times are just as applicable today. God says he changes not (Matthew 5:17–19). Jesus Christ did not do away with the Ten Commandments, and he expanded and reinforced the commandments and tenets of the Bible (Matthew 4:4, Matthew 5, 7, 19:17; Mark 10:19; Luke 18:20; John 14:15, 15:10; I John 2:3–4, 5:1–3; Revelation 12:17, 14:12, 22:14). All people are to keep the commandments and tenets of the Bible (I Kings 2:3, 8:34–40, 43, 57–61).

For individual human beings, everything is not lost for those who have erred. God is a loving God, and when an individual confesses his sins to God and stops doing bad things, then God is quick to forgive (Acts 2:38; I John 1:9; Ezekiel 18:21–32).

I have listed just the main problems. The people of the United States and the nation of the United States are condemning themselves because of the problems listed herein. The United States has declined and will go into captivity because God has turned his back on the United States. God will condemn and reject Israel (the United States) for not following his commandments (Jeremiah 31:35–37; Ezekiel 2, 3, 5, 6, 7). Many Israelites will flee the United States (Leviticus 18:24–30; Ezekiel 5:12).

By the time of Noah, people had gotten so evil that God destroyed the earth by water. As I have told you previously, there is a duality all through the Bible. So, at the end-time, people will have gotten so evil that God will destroy the earth the second time, except for the elect again. This time it will be by fire (Matthew 24:36–51; Luke 17:26–36; Isaiah 66:15–16; Revelation 20:9).

Anyone who causes one of God's people to go astray is condemned (Proverbs 28:10). In today's society you see many people mostly for profit reasons but also for other reasons trying to entice other people to do evil things.

Chapter VII
Emphasis on Schools and Education

A fifth event causing the decline and captivity of the United States is that just before the end-time there is great activity to see that everyone is educated—that everyone has a college education. If everyone gets a college education, then who will do the work that needs to be done? One doesn't need a college education to drive a truck, wash dishes, run a computer, sell goods, sort mail, or do thousands of other jobs. There are not enough administrative, executive, research, and highly technical jobs available to employ anywhere near the total number of college graduates.

As a consequence, what do we have? We have pressure put on Congress to create many more departments and agencies at taxpayers' expense so that those graduates can have jobs. And because those new graduates think that they are above doing manual labor, the United States has had to allow aliens (illegal or otherwise) to come into the United States to handle the manual labor type jobs. The United States is destroying itself. (Proverbs 1:5, 7; Hosea 4:6; James 1:5).

The schools are the saddest of institutions (Galatians 1:4). They are Satan's workshops. The politicians, under pressure to solve the problems of why the graduates cannot read, write, speak, or think, are pouring money like it was water into the school systems. They do this to get more votes for themselves. More money for the schools won't solve the education problem. The problem is that people with special interests have gotten control of the educational systems and are milking them for their own benefit. The college professors are more interested in promotions and writing books for money than in teaching truths. The more books and papers they write, the more attention they receive from their peers. The individual teachers are more interested in getting promotions and pay raises and fewer duties. They have their unions now, which takes up a considerable portion of their time, and they are so powerful that they are controlling the legislatures. The time could better be spent educating their pupils. The schools themselves try to outdo each other. They demand new buildings, new departments, the latest new equipment for them, new stadiums, new arenas–all to outdo the other universities for bragging rights.

Students are graduating now from high school and college who cannot read, write or perform simple mathematics and do not know history, geography, or social ethics. Much of their time is spent in fun activities such as painting, drawing, the arts, computer games, but mostly sports. The big thing is sports. What does sports have to do with education? Nothing. In the schools now, students must spend hours training for their sports activities and then spend many more hours running around in buses or planes all over the country to compete with someone. This is time they should be spending learning to become decent citizens. The whole promotion in sports is "winning at all costs." You hear the expression "Pride" spoken by athletes all the time. Pride is an abomination (Ezekiel 16:49; Isaiah 28:1; Job 35:12). Each person's thing is to outdo the other fellow, which is entirely un-Christian (Proverbs 29:23).

Centuries ago, the Romans brought individual heathens up from Africa to Rome to perform athletic events and to outdo each other and animals, for the sport and pleasure of those who could afford to go to the Colosseum. They even went so far as to hire people to kill Christians. Except for the killing of Christians, the United States is following the same pattern. If the promoters of sporting events can figure out a way to work it, the United States may see the killing of Christians within its borders in the near future (I Corinthians 8:1–2).

The schools are Satan's workshops, and they will be destroyed when Jesus returns to earth (Hosea 4:6; Psalms 50:16–17). Another interesting point to note is that when the heathen take over a country, the first thing that they do is kill the educated people. The heathen themselves recognize that modern education can be a big source of trouble. Most of the things that are taught in schools are for self-promotion and are contrary to what is in the Bible. The concept of education now is "how to make money," "how to get the best of the next guy," "how to promote yourself," and "how to impress other people." This is called pride and vanity, which are abominations (Job 35:10–13, 40:11–12; Ecclesiastes 2:1–11). The Bible says that no one can enter God's Kingdom unless he receives God's word as a little child (Luke 18:17). Very few high school or college graduates ever identify themselves as being like a little child. They would be laughed at by their associates.

In the schools, one learns to use flattery in order to win all that his heart desires—favors, money, power, promotions, awards. It is condemned (Daniel 11:21–22, 32–34; Proverbs 20:19, 28:23, 29:5). All is vanity, because when people die they are dust (Ecclesiastes 1:13–14, 18, 3:18–20).

The schools are graduating ignorant individuals (Isaiah 56:10–11), who learn how to pollute God's creation and redirect natural forces and learn ways to separate money from those who have it. The only knowledge that is worthwhile is revealed knowledge from God (Galatians 1:11–12; James 1:5; Job 4:17–21, 5:12–14, 12:17). It takes months of study of the Bible to obtain this knowledge, and anyone can get this knowledge. But most people are more interested in promoting themselves than getting true knowledge; thus only certain ones (the 144,000) can receive true knowledge (Luke 8:10; Exodus 28:3, 31:1–11). The wisdom of the world is foolishness (I Corinthians 3:18–21). Only one man in a thousand gets wisdom (Ecclesiastes 7:25–29). More and more, people are using fancy words and learning rapid-fire speaking. The schools and seminars teach that time is money and thus rapid speaking. You notice it especially in the media. A listener is not sure what the person says. As a matter of fact, the speakers probably don't know what they just said either (James 1:19). They are fools (Ecclesiastes 5:2–7; Proverbs 29:20). When a person speaks, he should think carefully about what he is speaking in order not to condemn or make a fool of himself.

Huge amounts of money are poured into the schools (I Corinthians 1:19–20). Most of it is wasted. Teaching about how and why the United States was founded has been eliminated from most schools. God has been eliminated from most schools. When Jesus returns to earth to set up his government, the universities and colleges will be eliminated—done away with. There will be instruction, but it will be based on the Bible.

The United States now could greatly cut costs by limiting to twenty percent the number of high school graduates that are allowed to attend colleges and universities. Just the brightest would be selected for engineering, management, and administrative training.

True wisdom is the fear of the Lord and departing from evil (Job 28:12–28). It comes from studying the Bible (Isaiah 28:9–14). God chose certain individuals to speak to through dreams (Job 33:14–16). God and his angels spoke to other individuals. All those people then recorded the information that was given to them. They are called prophets. That is how the Bible was written.

Because the schools have rejected God from their halls, God will turn his back on the United States.

Chapter VIII

The Enemies of the United States Will Eat Its Substance

A sixth event at the end-time that will precede the captivity of the United States, and which will be a cause of it, is that the enemies of the United States will eat the grain and meat produced in the United States (Leviticus 26:15–16; Deuteronomy 28:33; Ezekiel 6–7). The United States is sending its grain to heathen and Gentile countries at bargain-basement or subsidized prices, and in many cases it is giving it away.

Russia, China, Japan, and Korea especially are eating the harvests of the United States. This giving away of the substance is due to pressure from the farmers on Washington to make greater sales of farm commodities in order to get better prices for their farm products and thus greater income. The pressure and the wrong administrative decisions in Washington are resulting in the feeding of the heathen and angering of God (Jeremiah 5:15–17). This will devastate the nation of the United States just before the end-time (Leviticus 26). There is a duality all through the Bible. Prophecies for Israel of the olden times are mirrored or in effect for Israel in the modern day or end-time.

What the United States is doing is completely wrong. God controls the weather and whether it rains or doesn't rain, whether the sun shines or doesn't shine, and whether the wind blows or not. God said that he would give Israel (the United States) rain in due season and good crops as long as Israel obeyed his commandments (Deuteronomy

11:13–16). The communist and/or heathen nations would soon collapse if the United States didn't feed them. God would withhold the rain from the heathen nations so they would not get any crops. The United States is circumventing God's will for the earth. Because the United States is doing that, God will let the United States destroy itself (Ezekiel 6–7). The wrong foreign policies are building up the enemies of the United States. As a result, the administration in Washington thinks that the United States has to spend $300 billion a year on war and defense preparation, which is breaking the budget.

Another reason that the United States is destroying itself is the use of its substances such as grain for motor fuel rather than food, for which it was intended. As a result of all this the farmland of the United States will become as a desert (Ezekiel 6:14).

If the United States would just follow the Ten Commandments and tenets of the Bible there would be no need to spend $300 billion a year on defense. God said that he would protect the United States (Israel) from its enemies (Deuteronomy 20:3–4). But as long as the United States is playing God, God will cut off the rain in due season and soon there will not be enough food grown to feed the people of the United States. Thus starvation and plagues will result (Ezekiel 6–7).

The enemies will take over the United States (Deuteronomy 28:48–52; Leviticus 26:31–33; Ezekiel 7:21, 24). Of the Israelites in the United States that haven't died from the plagues and from violence, the few that are left will flee to other countries, where they will be harassed (Deuteronomy 28:62–68; Ezekiel 5:12–15). But this harassment will be only for a short while until Jesus returns to earth. When Jesus returns, the enemies of the Israelites will no longer eat the corn and other food products that are produced by the Israelites (Isaiah 62:1–9).

Chapter IX
Unlimited Immigration

A seventh event causing the destruction of the United States, and which is probably one of the worst laws of modern times, was the law that allowed the aliens who came into the United States in the past twenty-five years to get citizenship.

Nearly all of those peoples that have come into the United States in the past twenty-five years were heathen or Gentiles (I Chronicles 16:35). God condemns the mixing of those peoples with the people of Israel. They are not to be let into the house of Israel (II John 9:11). God also forbade the marriage of an Israelite to anyone who is not an Israelite (Nehemiah 10:30; Exodus 34:15–16; Genesis 24:3–4). Please refer to the books of Joshua, Samuel, and Kings in the Bible where God directed the Israelites to take over certain lands and, in doing so, kill every man, woman, and child of the heathen nations (Ezra 9:1–3).

In the nineteenth century and the first half of the twentieth century the administrations in Washington let into the United States many Gentile and heathen people. That was also wrong. The heathen and Gentiles who have come into the United States have brought their pagan religions with them (Matthew 6:7; Psalms 9:15). Israelites who accommodate those people by accepting their religions into their community cannot have any inheritance passed down from Joseph and Jacob. God commands the Israelites to destroy the pagan rites, rituals, and items of worship, such as statues, totem poles, carved animals, other carved objects, stone objects, and any other items of worship representing birds, sun, moon, or stars. They are an abomination (Exodus 34:10–16; Deuteronomy 7; Jeremiah 10:1–5; Numbers 15:13–16).

Policies adopted by the United States have let millions of strangers into Israel (the United States) and have permitted their customs, celebrations, religious activities, manners, and morals to continue on in the United States. This accommodation of those things is an abomination (I Corinthians 5:1, 10:20; I Thessalonians 4:3–5; Psalms 59:5–8, 79:6). One of the biggest mistake that the United States has made was adopting the affirmative action legislation that helped facilitate this accommodation (Ezekiel 11:12).

That is not to say that some strangers could not become a member of God's Kingdom, but in order to do so they must adopt the Ten Commandments of God and do them. If strangers (non-Israelites) come into the United States or any other Israelite nation, they must be laborers or supervisors of laborers (Isaiah 61:5–6). They cannot be rulers, supervisors, or soldiers, unless it is in a labor type capacity (I Chronicles 22:2–4; II Chronicles 6:32–33; Deuteronomy 31:12; Numbers 15:14–16). A nation cannot be divided and stand (Matthew 12:25; Mark 3:24; Luke 11:17). The United States is accommodating the heathen and Gentiles by not insisting that they learn the language, morals, and customs of the Israelites (Deuteronomy 31:16–18, 29). The United States is letting them have their churches, rituals, celebrations, and language. That is wrong, to allow them to do that. Gentiles who come into an Israelite nation may be allowed to stay provided that they receive instructions and follow God's commandments, but they will be servants and laborers (Joshua 9:4–27). No person should be permitted to hold a job or drive a car unless he learns to speak, write, and read the English language. No person should be allowed to vote unless he reads, writes, and speaks the English language (Leviticus 25:44–46).

Israelites are commanded not to take strange wives. Strange wives are those people who are not Israelites. If Israelites do take strange wives, they suffer condemnation (Ezra 10:1–19). Israelites who commit adultery or fornication with a non-Israelite will be destroyed (Numbers 25:1–9). The same goes for Israelite women who take strange husbands.

A divided nation is headed for destruction (Luke 11:17). At the end-time the United States will not demand that strangers in their midst adopt God's commandments, so as a consequence, the United States will be destroyed (Joshua 23:7, 11–16; Leviticus 26:31–33; Ezekiel 2, 3, 4, 5, 6, 7).

On a related matter, there is some effort now to adopt a "new world order" in which every nation abides by a fixed set of rules. That is an abomination. Israelite nations should have nothing to do with non-Israelite nations, with the exception of some trade activities. Those people who are promoting the "new world order" concept have no knowledge of what is in the Bible and with that attitude could not be accepted into God's Kingdom.

When someone enters or is invited into your home, that someone must abide by the rules of your home; otherwise that someone must get out. The same principle must be followed by a nation. The United States was established by God as a home for the Israelites.

Chapter X
Affirmative Action Laws

An eighth event and one of the biggest mistakes that the United States made was the passing of the affirmative action legislation (Luke 16:13–15). It is contrary to every biblical principle. When a man needs to hire a man or a man is seeking work, the biblical guideline is for the two to meet face to face, verbally agree on the terms of employment, shake hands, and that is it. There is employment (Matthew 18:18–20). The man doing the hiring in no way needs to accept someone he doesn't think can be acceptable as an employee. Also, if the employee does not measure up to what the employer thinks he should be, then the employer can dismiss the employee at will.

Under biblical concepts, there is no way that the hireling is to be in a position to tell the person doing the hiring what to do (Ephesians 6:5–9; Colossians 3:22–24; I Timothy 5:18, 6:1–2; Leviticus 25:43–53). Thus unions are an abomination. If the person doing the hiring becomes a despot, then God will see that he is destroyed (Malachi 3:5; Deuteronomy 24:14–15; Matthew 20:1–14).

Another fact of that antidiscrimination law is the mandatory hiring of women into executive, management, administrative, and other positions of authority (I Timothy 2:5–15). That is an abomination. God is the head of man; man is the head of woman. In every household, man is the head of the house—that is God's law (I Corinthians 11:3). Man is put on earth for certain functions, that is to build, to administer, and to rule, to provide for his home and family, and to fight and conquer. Women were put on earth to bear children, to guide them, to teach them, to nurture them to become sober, honorable men and women, and to keep up the home and cook the meals (I Timothy 2:11–15). Women as soldiers are an abomination.

The United States was founded, with God's help, to be an Israelite nation. Therefore, no one who is not an Israelite or no one who has not been converted to the precepts and tenets of the Bible should be permitted to be in a position of authority of any kind (Proverbs 29:2).

Any stranger—those who are heathen, pagan, or Gentile—who is living in an Israelite nation must be a laborer or, in some cases, a supervisor of laborers. They cannot be rulers, administrators, managers, or soldiers unless in a labor-type capacity (I Chronicles 22:2–4; II Chronicles 2:17–18, 8:7–9). Strangers in an Israelite nation may be bought and sold and treated as a possession (Leviticus 25:42–49). Israelites cannot be bought and sold.

Because affirmative action laws passed by Congress are directly contrary to God's commandments and tenets of the Bible and because men and women have abandoned their functions in Israel (the United States), God will turn his back on the United States.

The legislative halls of the states and the nation became infiltrated with elected officials who were not Israelites and by women who have abandoned their proper function. They outvoted the Israelites in the halls of Congress and the state legislatures. Thus the terrible laws were passed that destroyed the United States.

Chapter XI
Loss of the Panama Canal

The ninth step on the road down to the decline and captivity of the United States is the loss of the Panama Canal. God promised the children of Israel control of the seas and security and safety from their enemies, and the gates of their enemies, for as long as they obeyed the Ten Commandments (Genesis 22:17, 24:60; Deuteronomy 33:27–28; Isaiah 60:5). One of the gates of the world is the Panama Canal. The children of Israel, and specifically the United States and Great Britain, shall possess the gates of their enemies. This inheritance was passed on to Joseph, the father of Ephraim and Manasseh, whose descendants are Great Britain and the United States. The gates of the world are the Suez Canal, Gibraltar, South Africa, the Falkland Islands, and the Strait of Malacca and the surrounding area, which were at one time all controlled by Great Britain, and the Panama Canal, controlled by the United States. Great Britain is Ephraim, and the United States is Manasseh, both sons of Joseph.

Because in the last few years Great Britain and the United States have turned away from the tenets of the Bible, they are losing the sea gates (Deuteronomy 28:49–52). Great Britain still has Gibraltar and the Falkland Islands, but they may be lost before long. The United States has given away the Panama Canal by the ignorant people in Washington. At this writing, there is a movement in Congress to cancel the treaty that gave away the canal. If the United States can reverse what they have done, then the life of the United States can possibly be extended.

Chapter XII
Ten Common Market Countries

A tenth event in determining the end-time and destruction of the United States is the establishment of or revival of the old Holy Roman Empire in Europe. That is about to be accomplished in the form of a union of ten nations in western Europe, which will be the most powerful union of all time (Revelation 17:12–13). It is now coming together in Europe under the name of the European Economic Community, or EEC, with headquarters in Brussels, Belgium. There are twelve countries in the union now, which is supposed to get into complete operation in 1992. I expect Great Britain and Denmark to drop out of the union when it comes down to the final documentation of regulations. That will leave Germany, France, Belgium, the Netherlands, Luxembourg, Italy, Spain, Ireland, Portugal, and Greece as the ten. You will note that these are mostly Catholic nations. There will be great control from the church in Rome of this union (Revelation 17:1–6). The beast referred to in the Bible is the Holy Roman Empire to be resurrected again just before the end-time.

This union will be the greatest religious, economic, political, and military power of all time. It will be partially responsible for the decline and destruction of the United States and Great Britain (Deuteronomy 28:47–52), accomplishing what it could not do in World War II (Hosea 8:8–10). This union will also send its armies roaring down into the

Middle East, subjugating the nation that calls itself Israel now, as well as all the surrounding area (Zechariah 14:1–2).

This ten-nation union will control the affairs of the world for a short while. Then there will be dissension and turmoil within its ranks, presumably initiated by those who are not Catholic. The union will turn against the religious leader and the church at Rome in the last days (Revelation 17:16–18). The great whore referred to in the Bible is the Catholic Church at Rome (Revelation 17:1–7). The seven heads are the seven resurrections and eras of the Holy Roman Empire. When Jesus returns to earth, the "great whore" and its system will be destroyed (Revelation 14:9–10).

The revival of the Holy Roman Empire is described in Revelation 13. It is called the "Beast" and is the ten-nation EEC. This is the last or seventh revival of the Holy Roman Empire. The ten crowns are the ten nations of the EEC. It will have great power for and three and one-half years and will destroy or kill everyone and every nation that does not obey it. The second "Beast" with two horns is (1) the pope and the Catholic headquarters at Rome and (2) the Eastern Orthodox Church at Istanbul (formerly Constantinople). This "Beast" will give power and authority to the first "Beast." The dragon is Satan. The second "Beast" will perform miracles that will add acceptability and power to the first "Beast." All Europe will become united. This unity between the church at Rome and the eastern counterpart and the economic, political, and military power of the EEC will dominate everything on earth.

The Christians who have fled the United States into other areas of the world, including Europe, will be in subjugation and oppressed and will be slaves in their new locations (Luke 21:12). Many will have fled to Europe (Jeremiah 23:1–3).

While this development is one without the United States, it is included as one of the twenty-four points causing the destruction of the United States, because the United States aided and abetted the formation of the union chiefly through NATO. This proves how stupid the administrations in Washington have been. Then again, the rise of the Holy Roman Empire is part of Bible prophecy, and as Bible prophecy has always come true, perhaps the people in Washington had no control over their actions.

The effect of this union on the United States will be tremendous. What is left of the United States will be a basket case or, if you prefer, a banana republic. The United States will not be able to compete with the EEC. The EEC will control the United States financially and economically. The military establishment of the United States will be in disarray and virtually nonexistent, because it has forgotten how an Israelite nation must conduct itself, not only with affairs of war but in all other matters. The United States has forgotten how to conduct itself as an Israelite nation with respect to financial and trade matters. The pope and his entourage will conduct prayers and offer condolences for those that are left in the United States, just like they are doing now in Africa and Central America. The Israelites will have fled to Europe and the islands, leaving the heathen, the mongrels, and the Gentiles to rape the land.

The times just ahead will be very difficult and horrendous, for a short while. The EEC is supposed to get into operation officially in 1992; however, I think that it may be a little later, perhaps two or three years later. Big developments like that usually do not start up as scheduled. These things take time.

During the period of the existence of the EEC, it will send forces down into the Arabian Peninsula and control all that area, including Babylon (Iraq), Syria, Jordan, Lebanon, and the nation that calls itself Israel today (Jeremiah 50:9–10).

Chapter XIII

Trade and Financial War with the EEC and Asia

The eleventh event and another big factor in the decline and captivity of the United States is the financial and trade problems resulting from competition from the EEC countries, Japan, the rest of Asia, and other countries (Deuteronomy 28:49–51).

Because of the people's lust for money, pleasures, and power and the unions, the United States will not be able to compete with foreign countries; nor should we try. The economy of the United States will decline. Factories are closing in the United States, and in some cases the factories are moving their operations to another nation where there are no unions and labor costs are much lower.

It has been said that the workers in the United States have become lazy because of indulging in alcohol, drugs, sex, gambling, and riotous living (Romans 12:11; Proverbs 12:24, 18:9, 21:25; Ecclesiastes 10:18). Many mistakes are made in the factories because of this. For example, a factory worker who was not alert could forget to tighten a bolt and as a result a terrible accident could occur, killing or hurting many people. One never knows how many car, train, airplane, boat, or other accidents are the results of workers that were not alert. Awards by courts for damages greatly increase costs of production.

Because the United States, with its higher standard of living, is trying to compete with foreigners but cannot produce goods at less cost then foreign companies, the factories of the United States are losing sales and thus the United States is losing its factories and jobs. Because the factories of the United States are closing, the people are buying foreign-made products and as a consequence money is going out of the country. The trade deficit is ballooning.

Because the elected and appointed officials in Washington are sending billions of dollars each year out of the country to heathen and Gentile nations in the form of foreign aid, the United States is going bankrupt. As a result of this welfare, or buying of lovers as it were, the officials of the United States are having to go with their hands out to rich foreign countries that have money to loan, begging them to bail the United States out of its financial difficulties. The people of Japan, western European countries, and others are urged to buy U.S. Treasury notes and bonds, and as of this date they are doing that. If they should suddenly decide that they will not do it anymore, then the United States will be in real trouble (Hosea 7:9–13, 8:7–10). If a private person would borrow money to put into the welfare kitty, he would be carted off to an asylum. But apparently the officials in Washington think that they can do it. The officials in Washington are giving away billions of dollars each year to foreign countries, to the World Bank, to international monetary funds, and to the United Nations. This is all welfare and the United States is borrowing money to do it. Perhaps the taxpayers and voters of the United States will wake up someday and put a stop to it.

The schools of the United States will be no help. Instead of learning workmanlike to make things, to produce things, the graduates want to go to a university and after graduation get a job at a desk where they can have a nice, soft paper-shuffling job or a job flapping their lips. Those type jobs are going to disappear if there are no factories. Many new graduates want a job where they can have, immediately, a nice new expensive car, a nice new three-bedroom home with all the latest appliances, and expensive new clothes so that they can present themselves to the world in a manner they have dreamed about. They don't seem to realize that one has to work and save to get those things (Proverbs 21:25). Nothing comes without working for it (Proverbs 12:24). Wealth is accumulated by building or making things or growing things. Production-type jobs are disappearing in the United States. Service-type jobs don't provide wealth.

The United States will lose out in the trade and financial competition. As a consequence of the lust for immediate wealth and soft living, God will take away the inheritance promised to Israel (the United States). The United States will go into captivity (Amos 9:4–5; Ezekiel 6:9).

A contributing factor for the failure of the factories in the United States to compete with foreign factories is the high cost of liability insurance. This is partially the result of ignorant juries awarding huge sums on claims for damages and greedy lawyers pressing for more and more legal actions. The insurance companies are big business and always make sure that their rates are high to support their empires in the manner to which they are accustomed. Insurance has no place in God's planning for earth and is wrong. God protects those who obey his commandments from damages (Psalms 92:12–14; I Samuel 2:7).

Israel should not indulge in any association, trade or otherwise, with heathen nations. Joining the United Nations or any other type union is wrong. The subsidies that the United States provides for sale of produce to foreign nations are wrong. The United States, as Israel, has no obligation nor any God-given tenet to trade or deal with any heathen nation. The United States should have adopted a "buy American" policy long ago, and the United States would not then have any of the trade problems that we have now. Trade should *only* have been if the United States benefited from it. Trade with other Israelite nations would have been perfectly proper. The "new world order" that some people are promoting now is an abomination (I Chronicles 16:35; Psalms 9:15, 33:10, 59:5–8, 79:6–7, 135:15; Jeremiah 10;2, 25). Jacob is Israel, which is the United States, and it should never have gotten into the welfare for foreigners' schemes—or are they scams?—and if it hadn't, the United States would not now have any financial problems.

Free trade agreements with other nations are an abomination and part of the reason for the downfall of the United States.

The real problem is that the people of the United States have forgotten who they are. The Book of Ezekiel was written for Israel (the United States and Great Britain) especially, plus the other eight tribes of Israel as secondary (Ezekiel 3:1–4). Ezekiel 5, 6, 7 describes what will happen to the United States and also Great Britain. The prophecies of Ezekiel were for a time far off or, in other words, the time of the end (Ezekiel 12:27), now, and they were not for the period of time when Ezekiel was living.

Chapter XIV
The United States Will Buy Foreign Lovers

The twelfth event that is a serious development contributing to the decline and captivity of the United States is that the United States is making a whoremonger out of itself. The United States is buying friends all around the world.

The United States should not become friends with the heathen and Gentiles. Friendship with the world is being an enemy of God (James 4:4). This was addressed to the twelve tribes of Israel, so Israelite nations should not be lovers of strange peoples. Israel hired lovers (Hosea 8:7–10).

A nation is a collective unit and as such does the same things that an individual does. When an individual gives money to a stranger, it is to get a favor and thus the individual prostitutes himself. The United States has sent taxpayers' money to various and sundry foreign countries. Thus the United States becomes a buyer of lovers or a whoremonger when it does that. Just as a whore does not respect a person who buys her favors, so a nation that receives the money does not respect the United States when the United States gives them money. It is a matter of human nature to not respect those who try to buy favors. There are built-in instincts in man as well as animals, and this is one instinct that comes into play in this situation.

If the United States feels that there is a problem in another area of the world that is or is going to affect the United States's security, as an Israelite nation, the United States then should go in with all its might and fury and see that the thing that is bothersome is corrected, but it should not send money to try to bribe other people to correct the problem. Because the United States has become a coward or wimpish with regards to this, then God will turn his back on the United States.

The United States is condemning itself for buying favors from Egypt to keep the Suez Canal open and oil tankers running (Isaiah 31:1–3), and also from Assyria (Iran, Germany, Iraq, and Syria) in order to keep the heathen and/or communists out of the oil-supply region (Hosea 7:11–12) and to buffer against the heathen and/or communists. Egypt is also considered Assyrian, because Assyria conquered it at one time. Strangers are those peoples that are not Israelites. (The Israelite nations are covered in chapter 1.) Perhaps an explanation is necessary with regards to Germany. When the Israelites moved from captivity in the area of the Caucasian Mountains to western and northern Europe, many Assyrians, their captors, moved along with them. Also, some Israelites either forgot or disobeyed God's word not to marry outside of their tribe, and as a result mongrels were produced from those marriages. Anyway, the Assyrians and the mongrels stopped off in eastern Europe and eastern Germany. The Israelites wanted to get away from their captors so moved on into western and northern Germany and western and northern Europe. The western and northern Germans are considered Israelites, while the rest of Germany is Aryan (Assyrian). Thus Germany is a mixture. The fact that Germany is the main force, along with the pope at Rome, behind the beast (the EEC) causes Germany to be regarded as

Assyrian, even though the western and northern parts are considered Israelite territory. Thus when the United States goes to Germany for help in order to buffer against the heathen and/or communists and to bail the United States out of its financial and trade woes, it is going to Assyria.

There is an interesting item with regards to the tribe of Judah (the Jews) as relates to the United States and Great Britain. The father of the tribes of Ephraim (Great Britain) and Manasseh (United States) was Joseph. When Judah was a young man, most of his brothers became jealous of Joseph and wanted to kill Joseph; however, after Reuben intervened and prevented Joseph from being killed (Genesis 37:21–22) Judah succeeded in getting Joseph taken captive into Egypt (Genesis 37:26–28). Because Judah was the leader of his brothers, it was probably Judah who suggested killing Joseph. Those people who study the Bible know that there is a duality all through the Bible. At the end-time, Judah will again try to get Joseph (the United States and Great Britain) in trouble (Isaiah 9:21). Please note the difficulties the United States is in regarding the Middle East situation because of the support the United States has given for most of the things that Judah (the nation that calls itself Israel today) is doing. Ephraim (Great Britain) and Manasseh (United States) will be against some of the things Judah (the nation that calls itself Israel today) does, but Judah will demand money, support, and privileges. The United States and Great Britain, because of their greed for an oil supply, will comply, and thus the United States will buy lovers.

After the ten tribes of Israel separated from Judah, they became Israel. Judah and Benjamin then became the nation of Judah. For a great part of world history and most of Bible prophecy, the lost ten tribes are Israel. When Israel went into captivity at the hands of the Assyrians, the ten tribes lost their identity as Israel until the end-time—now. God gave them a new name (Isaiah 62:2, 65:15; Hosea 2:17). When Jesus returns to earth, then Judah and Israel will be reunited into one group at Jerusalem, called Israel (Revelation 7:4–8; 21:12; Mark 13:27). Because of the nation of Judah's sins, which were much worse than Israel's, Judah was scattered by God into all the heathen and Gentile nations and lost their status and name as a nation until the end-time (Jeremiah 23:1–7; Zechariah 7:14). At the end-time, now, many have migrated into Israelite nations and to Jerusalem.

The United States and Great Britain will go to Assyria (Germany, Iran, Iraq, Syria, and Egypt) for help with their problems (Hosea 8:7–10) and will be dependent on the Assyrians for their survival and thus captive. Look at who held U.S. and British citizens captive in Lebanon, Iran, etc.

An example of the sick thinking in the United States, brought about no doubt by the influence of the Sunday churches, is the policy of the United States of furnishing millions of dollars in aid to those countries that it thinks it has defeated in battle. A common joke around the world is to get into a war with the United States, then lose, then have your country rebuilt with money from the United States.

Chapter XV
Cowardice of the United States

The thirteenth thing and one of the saddest occurrences, not as one event but a growing cancer eating away the strength of the United States, is that the United States does not have the will to win wars anymore. This is reflected in the type of questions and harassment with which the media bombards the military establishment.

God commands the Israelites to follow the Ten Commandments. Because most of the people in the United States have turned away from God's commandments, God has turned his back on the United States and withheld the will to win (Leviticus 26:14–19). The United States has become afraid to assert itself or commit itself to winning and thus has become a coward and unworthy of God's help (Joshua 23:11–13).

Refer to the books of Joshua, Samuel, and Kings in the Bible. When the Israelites came out of Egypt, God commanded them to go into the land of Canaan, which was a heathen group of people, and to destroy every man, woman and child. The Israelites did just that (Numbers 31, 32; Joshua 8, 10, 11; Deuteronomy 2:33–35, 3). They were commanded to take the spoils for themselves, which they did. God's commandments to the Israelites were not for just those early times but for all times until the end-time (I Samuel 15:1–8).

God aided the United States (Israel) in the victory in World War II and earlier wars. At the end of World War

II, the will and morals of the United States began to decline. The turning point was around 1950 or shortly thereafter, when the decline was rapid and the United States ceased to be a Christian nation. The armies had won World War II, and some wanted to continue on into eastern Europe and Russia to liberate those people. The wimpish government in Washington turned coward and wouldn't let the armies do that. Because the military commanders who wanted to do that were not allowed to do so, the entire world has been suffering ever since. The Israelites of I Samuel, II Samuel, I Kings, and II Kings would have driven on to Russia and destroyed every vestige of heathenism in eastern Europe. If the United States had done that, God would have blessed it immensely. Perhaps the people in Washington wanted to save lives. Those that would save their lives shall lose them (Matthew 16:25; II Samuel 22:38–43).

The United States did not win the Korean War. It should not have been in that war. It had no interest there, except for the manufacturers of wars' death-dealing products and the bankers who get rich from war activities. But once the United States was in it, they should have ended it quickly by dropping an atomic bomb on the right place. There again the wimpish Washington authorities would not allow the commanders in the field to end it quickly or at least to drive on to China and secure the entire peninsula. As a result, there has been turmoil ever since in Korea, with great expense to the United States. For shame!

Again, the United States should not have gotten involved in the Vietnam War, but once the decision had been made to get involved, the war could have been ended in a day or two by dropping an atomic bomb in the right place. There again, the wimpish government officials in

Washington turned coward and would not let the soldiers win the war. Now God is letting the United States flounder in the morass that it has created for itself. The refugees that are coming into the United States are an abomination.

Again, if it was determined that the heathen that have taken over Cuba and Nicaragua were a security risk for the United States and should be destroyed, then the United States has failed miserably.

God let the United States develop the atomic bomb to save Israel (the United States and also Great Britain) in World War II. If the United States uses the bomb appropriately, God will bless the United States. The United States has lost track of who it is and why it is and is acting like a sickly coward.

God will assist any Israelite nation to win any war provided that the people of the Israelite nation follow God's commandments (Deuteronomy 1:28–30, 28:7; Exodus 23:27; Leviticus 26:6–8, 14–19). It was part of God's covenant and blessing to Israel. If the people of the United States would follow God's commandments, their enemies would turn and run away or else be destroyed. War is necessary to carry out God's plan for earth. Israelites went to war against the heathen and always won, except during those times when they turned away from God's commandments (Deuteronomy 28:14–68). When God stirs up an Israelite nation to war against a heathen nation, utter destruction is to be made—all men, women, children, and even animals if the Israelites so desire—of that nation (Numbers 31:1–18; I Samuel 15:2–33). Israelites, in accordance with God's covenant, may slay all those peoples that hate them (Esther 9:1–16; Joshua 24:8–13).

Not only nations but individuals are receptive of heaven-sent miracles or have one of God's people intercede for them, provided that they follow God's commandments (I

Kings 8:44–52; II Kings 1:10–12, 2:23–24, 4:32–41, 5:14). Nearly everyone has learned how David killed Goliath (I Samuel 17). God works in strange ways sometimes to accomplish his purpose on earth; for example, Samson, of the tribe of Dan, was enamored of a Philistine girl, which resulted in the destruction of many Philistines (Judges 13:24–25, 14, 15, 16). The Philistines were a heathen nation.

As long as the people of the United States follow God's commandments and pray to God, God would fight their battles for them—one soldier would whip a thousand (Joshua 23:3–10; II Chronicles 32:20–22). The United States should not be concerned with world opinion, but only with God's opinion (Isaiah 51:7–8). If any Israelites in any other area of the world would ask for assistance to oppose godless tyrants, then it would be the duty of the United States to help them. But the United States should not help any nation that is not Israelite. That is why the new world order and the United Nations that some are promoting is an abomination. Israel (the United States and Great Britain) is God's right hand by which God will accomplish his plan for earth (Jeremiah 51:19–23). The United States (Israel) inheritance, in part, was to control the world and destroy heathen nations who got out of line and evildoers (Deuteronomy 2:25, 28:10; Isaiah 60:10–12). The United States has only to believe and do.

It is completely wrong for women and heathen to be soldiers in an Israelite army, except in a labor-type capacity. Because the United States has accepted them in combat units and because the people of the United States mostly are not following God's Ten Commandments, it is doubtful that the United States will ever win another war.

God has turned his back on the United States. Thus the people of the United States will shake like a leaf before their enemies and cower in their homes. They will go into captivity, and the cities and land will be destroyed and made waste (Leviticus 26:27–39; Numbers 14:42–43). God's elect will be saved, and those that do not follow God's commandments will go to destruction. The Book of Ezekiel in the Bible was written specifically for the United States and Great Britain (Israel). That book tells what will happen to them. It was not written for Judah, except as an aside.

With regards to the failures of the United States in the Vietnam War and the Korean War, the United States should not have been in those areas. The United States was not protecting or defending itself or the territory of any other Israelite nation. It was to protect a heathen people and their territory, so God withdrew his support in those wars. The only outcome possible for the United States was defeat or a stalemate. If those had been Israelite nations and they had asked the United States for help, then the United States would have won the wars. It is doubtful that God would protect or support the United States if they went fighting for a heathen nation. God will protect the United States if they are protecting their own country or the interest of the country and they follow God's commandments (Joshua 7:12–13).

With the greatly superior technology that the United States has developed in the past, the United States would have success in any police-type actions that it may get involved in. For instance, they dominated the Panamanian forces in that police action. Yet they didn't really get the job done. The leader of Panama is languishing in the United States at taxpayers' expense, and Panama is still in turmoil. A true Israelite nation going in to protect their interests would have annihilated the populace and taken over the country. The United States didn't do that and thus were cowards (Joshua 8:24–26). Apparently the United States thought a police action was necessary in Grenada to protect their interests. They failed, as turmoil continues in the land of Grenada. There again, if the United States felt that they must go into a land to protect their interests, then they should have destroyed the land and taken it over.

Because of the cowardice of the United States, God has turned his back on the United States. The United States will go into captivity (Amos 7:17; Ezekiel 22:4).

Israelite nations and individuals should not conform to the affairs of the world. That is the way to destruction and death (Romans 12:2). There is a tendency now to run to the United Nations to get their approval and support for any type action. That points out the wimpishness of the United States. The United States should have nothing to do with the United Nations. There are many brave men and units in the armed forces of the United States who if left alone to accomplish their objective will do so. However, because of the deterioration of society and the wimpishness in Washington they are not allowed to do so.

Much thinking around the United States today, no doubt promoted by the Sunday churches, is that Jesus Christ was a man of peace. So many people and leaders of the United States advocate peace at any price. That is not in accordance with God's plan for the people on the earth (Matthew 10:34). Jesus said that he did not come to send peace but a sword.

God's chosen people, the United States (Israel), are God's right hand on earth to destroy the despots and tyrants of the world. Judah, the nation that calls itself Israel today, has never been in a position to do so, because they have been scattered, by God, to all the nations of the earth. Because Israel (the United States) has teamed up with the United Nations with regards to this matter rather than doing the job itself, Israel (the United States) has profaned itself and thus God will turn his back on Israel (the United States). Most of the nations of the United Nations are heathen and Gentile.

Chapter XVI
One-third Will Die from Plagues

The fourteenth event causing the destruction of the United States is that at the end-time one-third of the people of the United States will die from famine, pestilence, and plagues (Ezekiel 5:12–17, 6:1–12; Luke 21:11; Mark 13:19–20; Revelation 6:5–6, 9:15). Does anyone not believe that the AIDS crisis is the Bible prophecy in full bloom? Notice particularly Ezekiel 5:17: "pestilence and blood will pass through thee." Dealing in blood is an abomination, yet you see the hospitals, with assistance from the media and other agencies, promoting blood donations and transfusions (Acts 15:20). Governments are feverishly spending time and money to try to solve the AIDS crisis. It will do them no good. All the money and research will be wasted. Sickness is the result of not living in accordance with the principles of the Bible (Leviticus 26:15–16). The hospitals and rest homes are full of sick people. Also, there are many defective babies being born now because the people of the United States are not living in accordance with the Bible.

A contributing factor to the plagues is the wrong farm practices by the farmers. Farmers are putting huge amounts of chemical fertilizers and pesticides on their ground (Numbers 35:34). These poisons are getting into the food and into the people that eat that food. Our bodies are being poisoned by those chemicals. It is no wonder that the hospitals and doctors' offices are full most of the time (Amos 7:15–17).

Another contributing factor is that farmers of the United States are planting the same type of grains in the soil year after year, fencerow to fencerow. As a result the soil is being depleted of good nutrients and the good natural chemicals necessary to be in the food in order for our bodies to be in good health (Exodus 23:10–11). I have heard that good soil should have thirty-five chemicals in it to produce good food. The soil of the United States is now testing out with only less than fifteen of those natural chemicals. The natural chemicals get into the soil from the rains and winds. Thus the grains and meat that are produced on the farms of the United States do not have the proper chemicals in them for the people to have good health (Leviticus 26:26).

This lack of good food can also be attributed to lack of rain in due season or possibly too much rain (Leviticus 26:2–4; Ezekiel 14:12–13).

One hears that AIDS patients are in their bad condition because their immune systems have been destroyed. With good, healthy food over the years, they would not be in that condition. God provided the necessary vitamins and minerals in the soil so that people could have good health (Leviticus 26:2–5, 26). The body heals itself with the proper diet. Famine and pestilence go together. A person will have good health if that person eats well-rounded meals. Then, if you follow the Bible instructions regarding good health, pray for good health, and pray to recover from sickness, you will be well (James 5:13–16; I John 3–22). The guidelines on what is good to eat and what is not good to eat are in Leviticus 11 and Deuteronomy 14:3–21. A sleep time of eight hours is necessary.

It is good to eat meat and drink wine (Deuteronomy 12:15; I Timothy 5:23; Ecclesiastes 9:7). It is possible to live to 120 years of age provided one lives by every word of

God (Genesis 6:3). The lands of the United States have been overgrazed and overplanted until there is little food value left in the soil. The farmers and ranchers should return to the Bible instructions on proper farming practices. Crops should be rotated, and the land should be left idle every seven years so it can renew itself (Exodus 23:10–12). The rains and winds bring down the minerals to the lands to restore them (Leviticus 19:19, 25:2–4).

Another factor in the sickness of the United States is that what few vitamins and minerals that are in our grains coming from the farms are being destroyed by the food processors in their manufacturing process (Leviticus 26:16). God did not create humans to be sick. The people are doing it to themselves by their practices.

The Israelites while they were in Egypt ate meat, fish, melons, cucumbers, leeks, onions, and garlic, so those things are good for a person to eat (Numbers 11:5). Many people are turned off by some of those items. No wonder they are sick. There are other things that are good to eat, and things that should not be eaten, but I don't want to get into depth on that here. There are many good books on nutrition. The Bible reference as to what is not good to eat is Leviticus 11. If people eat things that should not be eaten, then they are going to get sick.

Another abominable practice is the dealing in blood. The Bible says that it is an abomination to ingest blood (Deuteronomy 12:16). Blood is used in some foods, but the worst thing is the blood transfusions being performed in the hospitals. The lifeblood of a person should not be used in a commercial way, but only for the purpose of sustaining the life of that person. Otherwise one is acting as God, which is an abomination. Dealing in blood is a sign of the end-time (Ezekiel 5:17). At the end-time, people will think they are doing good things—the Gospel according to man's, not God's thinking. A person's blood is his lifeblood and is unique to that individual only, regardless of what some doctors think (Genesis 9:4–6; Leviticus 17:10–14).

King Asa of Judah died from diseased feet because he sought a physician's help instead of God's help (II Chronicles 16:12–13). People can be cured by eating the right things and praying to God for help and following the Ten Commandments. God in his wisdom has provided plants, flowers, fruits, grains, herbs, soil, etc., that will keep people healthy and will cure anything, provided one knows what to eat and use. Many of the physicians don't want people to know about those things, because if people eat the right things and heal themselves, physicians and pharmacists can't make money. Doctors are necessary in certain instances, such as setting broken bones or for snake or insect bites, but they are not God's favorite people. Yet society today has exalted the doctors. You hear many various phrases about how doctors know best. Instead of a trip to your doctor, a trip to your neighborhood health food store could solve many health problems.

On a related matter, the doctors seem to think it is good to prolong life in a vegetable state. That is wrong. There is a time to be born, a time to live and work, and a time to die. God determines that. Some doctors are assuming that they are greater than God. They will suffer the wrath of God for it. If a person cannot find pleasure in being alive, there is no point to being alive like a vegetable. Besides, that is a heavy burden to all those around him. If this policy is not changed, and considering the self-serving, groveling attitude of some politicians it probably won't be changed, the United States will go broke providing catastrophic medicare for all those getting sick. There are many blind and lame in the United States, apparently because of sins of their fathers or themselves. The United States spends billions of dollars to educate and to provide special facilities such as entrances to buildings and transportation. This is a sign of decadence. The Israelites do not consider those people as God's people (II Samuel 5:8). The doctors and pharmacists stock the drugstores and hospitals with many chemicals that they think will cure most ailments from which they make fantastic profits. People should realize that God provides natural remedies in foods and plants. For example, a cure for boils is stated in II Kings 20:7.

If people sin, they will suffer sickness (Leviticus 26:14–16). Adulterers are prime candidates for sickness (II Chronicles 21:12–19). Sickness and plagues even come to kings if they do wrong things (II Chronicles 26:18–21). Prayer and fasting can cure some sickness (Mark 9:29).

Also note that all who have a communicable disease are to be put out of society or quarantined (Numbers 5:1–4). This probably won't happen, because there is getting to be so many of them and they all vote; thus the politicians in Washington, being more interested in votes than God's will, will do nothing about it. Another interesting point is that God will put evil diseases on all those people who hate the Israelites (Deuteronomy 7:15). With all the non-Israelites now coming into the United States, at the request of Congress and the administration, bringing with them their own diseases, one thinks that God is laying the horrible diseases of Egypt on the United States. Some of those new aliens are antagonistic toward or hate the people of the United States (Israel). Many want to retain their own customs, rituals, religions, morals, etc. This cannot be done (Jeremiah 10). God will be very angry for allowing this pollution to happen. Not only will the

United States go bankrupt trying to provide medical facilities and care for those people, but God will bring plagues down upon the United States for polluting the country. The United States was created especially as a home for Israelite peoples, and the heathen are not to be allowed to pollute it. Because the United States has allowed it to happen, plagues will consume and destroy the United States (Deuteronomy 28:15–68; Ezekiel 5, 6, 7).

In times of great famine, people will eat people as happened in Samaria years ago (II Kings 6:25–29). At the end-time men will eat their sons and sons will eat their parents (Ezekiel 5:9–10). If people sin and commit whoredoms, there will not be rain and thus no food to eat (Jeremiah 3:1–3; II Chronicles 7:12–14). However, if people change their ways and pray for rain, rain will come (James 5:17–18; Leviticus 26:2–4; II Chronicles 6:26–31). God can turn on rain and turn off rain according to the acceptance of God's commandments by a nation (I Kings 17:1, 18:1). People will prosper and be in good health if they keep God's commandments (I Kings 2:3–4), eat the proper food (Leviticus 11; Deuteronomy 14:1–21; Proverbs 24:13), and pray for the right things (I Kings 3:9–13, 8:33–39; Deuteronomy 27, 28:1–4, Deuteronomy 29, 30). God controls the weather (Jeremiah 51:16), along with having made everything in the universe (Jeremiah 51:15). Thunder is God speaking (I Samuel 7:10; Job 37:4–5).

Another abomination is the programs of genetic engineering that are being pushed in the universities and research plants around the country. Man cannot improve on what God has done (Genesis 1:24–25; Leviticus 19:19). The results of this engineering will cause all kinds of sickness in people.

There is much talk now about socialized medicine or a national health plan for the United States. That would be a disaster. With one-third of the people dying from pestilence and plague, one-third dying from violence, and the remaining one-third so debilitated that they wish that they were dead but cannot die, the country would soon be bankrupt.

Some of the worst decisions contributing to destroying the health of the people of the United States are made by people with the power to help make the United States a healthful country. For example, mercury is one of the deadliest poisons in the world, yet dentists are putting mercury in silver dental fillings in people's mouths. About 50 percent of a silver filling is composed of mercury. The mercury leaks out when people chew and causes many health problems. Also, fluoride, which cities and towns put into their drinking water, is a poison. It is estimated that more than 10,000 Americans a year are dying of cancer caused by fluoridated drinking water. The reference with regards to this is a book titled *Fluoride, the Aging Factor*, by John Yiamouyiannia (Health Action Press, 6439 Taggarts Road, Delaware, OH 43015).

In summary, God promised the United States rain in due season and bountiful harvests, which the United States had had in the past, but God will cut the rain off because the United States has turned away from God's commandments (Deuteronomy 11:13–17, Deuteronomy 27, 28, 29, 30; Ezekiel 6, 7). In addition to one-third of the people of the United States dying from famine and plagues, one-third will die from violence, and most of the remaining one-third will be in such bad shape that they will wish they could die, but they cannot (Ezekiel 5:12–17). Some will scatter to the heathen and Gentile nations, where they will be persecuted. Some will go to other Israelite nations. This all will be in the last days.

Chapter XVII
One-third Will Die from Violence

The fifteenth event that will be ongoing at the end-time is that one-third of the people of the United States will die from violence (Ezekiel 5:12–17, 6:12; Revelation 6:4). You can see this in process now. People are shooting other people in the streets. Airplanes are falling out of the sky. Ships are sinking in the seas, rivers, and lakes. Many horrible abominations will occur (Ezekiel 7).

With the growth of television and education for everyone, those who are unstable are learning the know-how to expend their pent-up hatreds in ways to harm those who they think are oppressing them. Also, shortly you will see terrorist activity grow in the United States. One of the biggest mistakes the United States ever made was to invite all the foreigners to come over to attend the colleges and universities in the United States. Most of those people are of a different ideology and many return to their countries with resentments and use their knowledge in an adverse way against the United States. Most heathen cannot understand the ways of the United States, an Israelite nation, or at least cannot accept the ways, and thus there is a natural resentment (Ezekiel 21:12).

Workers in the United States are coming to work stoned or tired out, and as a result, mistakes are made in manufacturing of products, repairs, and maintenance of machines, which later destroy, with loss of life. People are so wrapped up in their personal pleasures that they make mistakes on the job. For example, a person will forget to tighten a bolt on an airplane or a car or a train and an accident results. This type thing will get worse.

It is sad that the munition makers and manufacturers of machines of war have such influence in Washington that the United States is spending $300 billion a year for war preparation in a time of peace. That is completely wrong. There will never be an atomic war between the superpowers. God would not permit it. People cannot seem to realize that God controls which nations are to grow and which are to be destroyed (Zechariah 12:9; James 4:12; Amos 9:8). In an atomic war all people, including God's elect, would be destroyed, and he would not allow that to happen (Matthew 24:22; Mark 13:20). God permitted the use of the atomic bomb on Japan because apparently there were no Israelites in Japan. There was no way that the United States could have lost World War II to Japan. The United States is Israel, and Japan is heathen. God protects the Israelites from the heathen, except in those cases when the Israelites turn their back on God. The same goes when the Israelites are at war against the Gentiles.

Yet the Bible says that at the end-time one-third of the people of the United States will die of violence. How can that be? Because the United States has turned its back on God. People are being shot in the streets; they are being shot and stabbed in the homes; they are crashing in planes, cars, trains, and boats. Terrorist activity by angry people sneaking across the borders will increase. A bomb in a briefcase can kill many. The streets of the United States will become battlefields and unsafe. The police cannot be everywhere, and budget restraints will not permit more police. That is how many people will die (Ezekiel 11:6–8).

This brings us to the last one-third of the people of the United States. The rest of the people will be so frightened and harrassed that they will flee to other countries (Deuteronomy 4:26–31; Isaiah 10:3). This will be the Israelites who cannot tolerate what is going on in the United States (Ezekiel 11:9–18). However, as they will be strangers in a new land, some will be in heathen nations, some will be in Gentile nations, and some will go to other Israelite nations, where many will suffer hardships and some will be killed (Ezekiel 5:12–17). Some will suffer eating and health problems in a strange land, because of strange food and lack of medical attention. Many will wish that they be dead but cannot die, and many will die (Ezekiel 6:12; Revelation 9:3–6, 14:9–11).

Because the courts of the United States do not execute judgment speedily and allow endless appeals and delays, evildoers are encouraged to do more evil and commit more violence. Thus the United States is destroying itself (Ecclesiastes 8:11–13).

Men will commit violence against one another through silly wars or through race or religious riots (Isaiah 3:25). Anger and wrath bring death to a person (Job 19:29). Everyone will die for their owns sins—children shall not die for their father's sins (II Chronicles 25:3–4). Death is sleep until the resurrection (I Kings 1:21). God charms (speaks to) serpents, animals, spiders, etc., so that they will not bite a person, if that person obeys the Ten Commandments (Jeremiah 8:17; Amos 9:3; Ecclesiastes 10:11).

If the people of the United States would change, turn around, and follow God's Ten Commandments, then they would be safe from harm (Leviticus 26:6–8, 21–22).

There will be a very few, called the elect, who will be saved from all the end-time tribulation and will be taken to a safe haven for three and one-half years, until Jesus returns to earth (Mark 13:27; Revelation 12:13–17). Those will be the 12,000 from each tribe of Israel. As the United States is only one tribe, there will be only 12,000 from the United States. (Those are identified in Revelation 14:1–5.)

Actually, it will be considerably less than 12,000, because many of the elect will have died previously—in previous decades and centuries. Those that have died previously plus those currently living will total to 12,000.

Chapter XVIII

Upset Weather and Earthquakes

The sixteenth event that points to the end-time is the upset weather. Make no mistake about it—God controls the weather (Leviticus 26:3–4). There are witnesses to actual events of one farm receiving bounteous rainfall and across the road there was none (Amos 4:7). It follows the tenets of the Bible, where they will have rain in due season when they follow the commandments of the Bible (Deuteronomy 11:13–15; Leviticus 26:3–5). At the end-time there will be upset weather. There will be too much rain in some places to drown out and flood the lands so that no crops will grow (Deuteronomy 11:16–17). There will be snow out of season in different places. There will be hail that will ruin crops in different places (Revelation 8:7; Ezekiel 38:22; Isaiah 30:30). There will be hot days in winter and cold days in summer.

There will be earthquakes in places that have never had earthquakes before, and there will be devastating earthquakes (Matthew 24:7; Mark 13:8; Luke 21:11; Revelation 6:12–17).

During the drought of 1988–89 one wondered if anyone was praying for rain. If they were and they were not getting rain, then they must not have been living according to the commandments of the Bible. God is a loving God for those who obey his commandments (James 5:17–18; I John 3:22).

At the end-time, instead of rain, dust storms will destroy the farmlands of the United States (Deuteronomy 28:24).

Before the upset weather and earthquakes occur, those who follow the commandments of the Bible will be persecuted (Luke 21:12). There have been claims that this has already happened in the United States. This persecution will be done by Satan's workers based on the commandments of men (government officials) rather than commandments of God.

A revolting development in the United States is the use of grain, grown by farmers in the United States, to run cars. When God created the universe, he provided rich lands so as to raise grains to feed the human race. To take those grains and make alcohol fuel out of them is so stupid and un-Christian that we wonder how anyone could propose such an idea. The by-product from that action is also used in an un-Christian manner (Isaiah 65:4, 66:17; Leviticus 11:7; Deuteronomy 14:8). There is fencerow to fencerow planting of the same crops, with no resting of the soil. As a consequence of farmers' not following the tenets of the Bible, God will shut off rain in due season (Leviticus 25:3–4).

The destruction of property and people from earthquake, tornadoes, and hurricanes will greatly increase despite the efforts of the media and government to defeat the devastating effects of those natural disasters. Great amounts of time and money are spent on efforts to warn and protect people from those natural disasters. It will all be to no avail. God controls the weather and actions of nature, and there is nothing that human beings can do about it (James 4:12; Amos 9:8; Micah 5:14; Ezekiel 5:16, 6:3, 25:7; Jeremiah 12:17, 13:14, 15:7).

Those who follow the tenets of the Bible will have rain in due season (Zechariah 14:16–19; James 5:17–18). Because the people of the United States have turned away from the commandments and tenets of the Bible the land will become desolate.

Chapter XIX
Stepped-up Peace Activity

The seventeenth event is that in the last days there will be much activity to secure peace among nations and among tribes. Diplomats and leaders of countries will run all over the world talking peace and sitting in on peace conferences and trying for agreements between nations and tribes to stop fighting. Peace, peace, and there is no peace, and there will not be any peace (Ezekiel 7:25), because Satan is ruling the world now until Jesus returns to earth (II Corinthians 4:3–4; John 18:36; Revelation 12:7–9).

Because of increased education and communication activities, everyone knows what everyone else is doing. Each has his own special interests to promote and thus counters with his own special proposals. With advanced electronics for spying and sale of national secrets by traitors, each nation thinks that they can eventually outdo the other nations and thus will not agree to anything unless their special interests are favored. Huge amounts of money and time are spent by the people in Washington on this matter, and it will be all to no avail. Everyone talks about peace, but there cannot be any peace because very few people follow the Ten Commandments anymore (Psalms 119:165). There can be no peace during the present world (Matthew 10:34). Only at the second coming of Jesus can there be peace (Revelation 21:4).

Peace efforts will be a failure (Isaiah 33:7–9), because there can be no peace for the wicked (Isaiah 48:22). Under

Satan's rule now, all nations are wicked at the present time, including the United States. All nations could get along with each other if they would forget their lusts for power and money. Israelites shall not abhor Arabs and Egyptians (Deuteronomy 23:7), and most do not. Also, Arabs and Egyptians and others should respect Israelite nations (Genesis 27:29). God commands it.

The tribe of Judah (the Jews) has been scattered to all the nations of the world because of their abominations. In the latter days, at the end-time, Judah will return to Jerusalem, which is what they are doing now (Jeremiah 12:14–17). The United States (Israel) has healed the hurt of Judah slightly by providing billions of dollars each year in foreign aid to Judah, the nation that calls itself Israel today (Jeremiah 6:14, 8:11).

Satan roams the earth and devours whomever he can now. However, God protects his elect and the Ark of the covenant (I Samuel 2:3–10, 5), and he regulates what goes on around the earth to a certain extent. If any nation gets out of line, God stirs up another nation to bring it to its knees, as happened in World War II. It has been that way all through history. As long as there are lust and greed in the world, there can be no peace. Everyone is proclaiming peace, peace, but there is no peace (Jeremiah 6:14).

God is keeping his hand off the affairs of the world now generally, except to protect his elect, to protect the Israelites, and to prevent any despot from destroying his world. The Lord God is not a God of peace of the world as we know it now, but of division (Luke 12:51). When Jesus returns to earth, then we will have peace.

Chapter XX
Stepped-up Sunday Church Activity

The eighteenth event pointing to the end-time is that there will be great activity by the churches to promote themselves, their brand of Christianity, to get new members, to get members to contribute more funds for new church buildings, new activity centers, new camps, and new classrooms. You see many new beautiful church buildings being built. The different denominations seem to be trying to outdo each other. If they can get a bigger and more beautiful church building, they feel that they can get more members and thus more funds to build more things. They get buses to take their members to camps they have set up for recreation purposes. "Vanity, vanity, all is vanity." Most of the activity is by Sunday churches but churches that meet on other days get into the act also.

Most of the churches are Satan's churches (Galatians 1:1–12). Do they teach what Jesus said and the message presented in the Bible? Most of what they teach is about the person of Jesus or what they think he was or is (Matthew 7:15; Romans 10:1–3; Titus 1:10–11).

Many new religions and churches are being established. Money seems to be the basis for the establishment of those. There is a proliferation of TV evangelists and radio evangelists. If one thinks he has a better idea, he can just get a radio spot or TV spot (Matthew 24:11). People are able to receive millions of dollars in contributions. Those sending their money to these folk will receive no good from it, except for a temporary soothing syrup so that they feel good. It is a waste of money.

Many have the wrong idea concerning tithing and whom to give it to. Tithing is 10 percent of the increase in your worth each year (Leviticus 27:32; Deuteronomy 14:22–25). If your cattle have reproduced so that you have twenty more cattle than last year, then your tithe would be 10 percent, or two cattle. If your income this year was $5,000 more than last year, then your tithe would be $500. You don't tithe on your gross income each year, but only on your increase. If you don't have an increase each year, then you should examine your life-style and determine why you are not living according to God's way of life and change your way of living. God rewards those who obey him (Deuteronomy 28:1–8). Those who give their tithes to anyone other than God's church are doing so in vain (Exodus 22:20).

In the later days there will be many false prophets (I John 4:1; Luke 21:8; II Corinthians 11:13–15; I Timothy 4:1–2; Matthew 24:5). Most are preaching what their audience likes to hear rather than Jesus' message (Titus 1:10–16; Colossians 2:8). Much wordiness, dressing in robes and sashes, and glitter is presented for show by the churches, all for naught (Luke 20:46–47; Matthew 6:7; Jeremiah 23;1–2; Mark 12:38–40).

A good way to tell whether a church is a true church of God or not is to see what customs and holidays they observe (Matthew 24:24; Leviticus 23). Are they God's holidays and sabbaths as stated in the Bible, or are they pagan rites and holidays? Jesus did away with the animal sacrifices and circumcision, but not the Holy Days, nor the commandments. More and more energy, money, and time is being spent by Sunday churches on Christmas, Halloween, Valentine's Day, and other pagan activities (Jeremiah 10:2–5; Deuteronomy 18:9–12). One activity that has questionable merit is the missionary activity. Much money and time is consumed on this, to no benefit. To be a true missionary, first one must know God's word. Very few know God's word. Proof that missionary activity is questionable is the fact that most of the countries where missionaries have gone have turned to violence. Most of the people don't even know or remember the Sabbath Day. That is Saturday. Nor do they keep the annual sabbaths. Jesus and his disciples observed Saturday as the Sabbath (Exodus 20:10, 31:13–18; Mark 1:21, 6:2). God's people observe Saturday as the Sabbath Day. That is how to tell whether a church is a true church of God or not.

Many people think such things as eating meat are wrong. Eating meat is not wrong. Jesus ate meat (I Timothy 4:3; Luke 15:23). A little wine is also good for an adult, but no one should get drunk (I Timothy 5:23). Much is made by politicians and others of how much money is given to a church—reporting to the IRS and to the media. When one gives to God's church it is to be in secret (Matthew 6:3–4) and only known to God himself and God's church. Making and selling statues is big business now, but please be reminded that no graven image shall be brought into a home, nor shall you bow down or worship a graven image. It is an abomination (Deuteronomy 7:25–26). "Those who sacrificeth or tithes to any save the Lord shall be destroyed" (Exodus 22:20).

Most of the people of the United States have forgotten their heritage. Most think that they are Gentiles (Jeremiah 50:6, 17). Because the people of the United States have forgotten their heritage, God will turn his back on the United States. The white people who settled the original thirteen colonies were Israelites and God's people. The descendants of those people and the descendants of those people who came in later from the British Isles, France, Belgium, the Netherlands, Norway, Sweden, Denmark, Finland, Luxembourg, Switzerland, Austria, the Baltics, and western Germany are Israelites and God's people. They are not Gentiles. Other people who, unfortunately, have been allowed to enter the United States are the Gentiles and heathen (Isaiah 42:1–6).

Satan knows that he doesn't have much time left, so he is working feverishly now to divert people away from the tenets of the Bible. Satan is the angel of light, glamour, glitter, frowardness, and boasting (II Corinthians 4:4, 11:13–15). That is what we have in the society of the United States today (Deuteronomy 32:20).

At the end-time there will be much activity sponsored by churches and preachers. Almost every event of any magnitude is clothed in religion in vain. Either the leader stands before the audience and prays for success or he gets the entire audience involved in prayer. Like the Pharisees and Sadducees and other hypocrites, they think that by much praying God will hear. It is all in vain (Matthew 6:5–7). Prayer to be heard should be in secret. The radio and TV preachers are big business and are vanity. Sports events, schools, and business meetings are begun with prayer, all to no avail (Luke 11:43–44).

God does not change. The commandments and tenets in effect in the old days are also in effect nowadays. Most people will get a chance after the resurrection to follow the commandments and tenets of the Bible and, if they do, to become saved.

Chapter XXI
Travel To and Fro

A nineteenth item that points to the destruction of the United States just before the end-time is that there will be much travel to and fro (Daniel 12:4). Many people now have a home in one part of the country and fly to work in another part or other parts of the country. Also, people who have retired and those who have vacation time think that they just have to go somewhere—anywhere, it seems, just go somewhere. They are not satisfied to stay at home and learn new things by reading or visiting neighbors or to work around their yard and enjoy the flowers, birds, and garden. Travel is also a way to shed all responsibilities.

So much of the travel pertains to entertainment, that would be best if never said, shown, or otherwise made available. Most is lust for pleasure, notoriety, or gain (Isaiah 47:8–11; Luke 8:14). All kinds of promotional activity is done by airlines, trains, hotels, motels, casinos, and others to get more people to travel and spend money with them.

Much of the travel pertains to church-sponsored activity—meetings, retreats, conventions, etc.—to try to learn more about the Bible and Jesus Christ (Amos 8:12). Only the elect have the truth and the answers. Many will spend great amounts of time and money to attend to those things, to no avail, except perhaps for an emotional lift.

Mountains, trees, and lakes in one part of the country generally look the same as those in another part of the country or world. When Jesus returns to earth, the scenery will be rearranged so you will not recognize it (Revelation 6:14, 21:1).

With all the promotional activity by the media of things to do, probably many travel because they can indulge in immoral activity and not be noticed by their neighbors and friends. Also, many may be embarrassed to remain around home when people ask them why they are not going on vacation.

Those who do most of this activity are the administrators and managers who seem to be constantly going to seminars and various meetings to receive or put out the latest information concerning their particular activity or perhaps to share who knows what. Mercenaries with an "ax to grind" for political or whatever purposes contribute heavily to this "to and fro" activity. The elected officials seem to think that they have to be constantly traveling to somewhere, it seems mostly for puffery. All this activity will be to no avail (I Corinthians 1:19–20, 3:18–19; Jeremiah 2:36).

There isn't much time left for this "to and fro" activity. When Jesus returns, restrictions will be mandated for airplanes, trains, ships, and cars. Generally, travel "to and fro" will cease except to and from Jerusalem. Airplanes, ships, trains, and cars may even be completely done away with in some areas (Zechariah 14:16).

Much travel "to and fro" is a firm indication that the end of civilization as we know it is near (Joel 2:9).

Chapter XXII
God's People Will Be Persecuted

A twentieth item spotlighting the end-time and decline of the United States is that there will be stepped-up persecution of God's chosen people (Hebrews 11:35–38; Revelation 12:12, 13:7). There has always been persecution of God's people, but there will be more of it at the end-time. Those people who follow the Ten Commandments will be shunned, made fun of, hated, mistreated by authorities, and even killed (Luke 21:12–18; II Corinthians 4:8–9; Matthew 5:25; Luke 12:58). They will be discriminated against with regards to employment and other things (Mark 13:9–13). It is happening now in the United States. Those people can recite many instances, and it will get worse. All through history those people have been mistreated and killed. The apostles were beaten, jailed, and killed. Many people will speak evil of the Israelites (Isaiah 60:14–15).

The Gentiles have always thought of Israelites as being strange, because the Israelites did not follow the pagan and evil customs of the Gentiles and the heathen (I Peter 4:3–4). However, the Israelites are to be a light to the Gentiles (Isaiah 49:6). A light at the end of a tunnel, as it were—out of darkness into salvation for those Gentiles who desire salvation.

Common terms generated by the heathen and Gentiles against the Israelites are *bigots* and *racists*. This is because the true Israelites follow the tenets of the Bible and do not approve of the activities of the Gentiles or heathen or associate with them. Israelites should not be ashamed to be called racists or bigots but should be glad and rejoice. It should be a badge of honor. The Gentiles and heathen reviled Jesus and his disciples the same way (Isaiah 51:7–8, 53:3). The Israelites of today who follow God's commandments and are persecuted are in good company. Any person who follows the Ten Commandments and God's teachings through his apostles, prophets, and disciples is subject to being called those things. Why? Because this is Satan's world and under his control now for an additional short time only, until Jesus returns to earth to rule. When Adam and Eve sinned, Satan was allowed to run to and fro on earth devouring all that he could. This was permitted by God up to a point, as long as God's elect were not hurt and as long as God's plan for the Israelites was not hurt. When Jesus returns, Satan's followers will be destroyed (Acts 3:23; Revelation 20:7–9).

After the United States goes into captivity for a short time, God's people will be persecuted much worse, in that those who do not have the mark of the beast will not be able to buy and sell (Revelation 13:16–17). Those that have the mark of the beast will be able to hold jobs and buy and sell. God's people will not be able to do so. With the invention of computers, it appears that the mark of the beast will be a number entered into a computer system, such as a Social Security number. Only those people who are approved would be able to have a number. If the authorities in control of the EEC do not approve of you for having a number, then you will not be able to hold a job or buy or sell. Who is the beast? The beast is the EEC, a revival of the Holy Roman Empire, soon to be put into place. Some say it will begin in 1992 (Matthew 24:9).

An explanation of why this persecution of the Israelites will exist may go back to early history. Jacob was the father of the Israelites. Esau was Jacob's brother and sold his birthright to Jacob for a mess of pottage. Esau was very angry because Jacob was given the birthright and blessings, and he demanded a blessing of his own from his father, Isaac. Isaac also blessed Esau and his generations with the fatness of the earth (good land, fruit, wine, sheep, and cattle) and dew (rain) of the heaven. I think that this fits in with Esau's descendants in Greece, Italy, Spain, Portugal, the Balkans, Iran, and Egypt. Those areas have been blessed with those things, and thus these people are considered Esau's descendants. Esau took wives from the tribe of Hittites, who are the black people, and because of that lost favor with Isaac and Rebekah (Genesis 26:34–35) and that was the key as to why he lost the birthright and inheritance from Isaac and from God. Esau also took a wife who was a daughter of Ishmael, the Arab people (Genesis 28:8–9). Esau is Edom (Edomites) (Genesis 36:1); however, Edom is a desert area. Originally Esau and his descendants probably did occupy Edom and then they migrated. Esau vowed to kill Jacob (Genesis 27:41), but Jacob escaped to another area. Later they made up (Genesis 33:1–16). Perhaps there is still resentment by the descendants of Esau toward the descendants of Jacob and they will try to get back at them at the end-time.

Dinah, Jacob's daughter, was violated by a Canaanite, and because of that Jacob's sons slew all the Canaanite men of that area (Genesis 34). God approved that slaying. So you can see that there was anger and resentment between the different peoples in early times as well as now.

Times will get so bad in the United States that those who follow the Bible and God's word may be beaten or killed and nothing will be done about it. This is beginning to be done now in the United States and in some cases is being kept quiet. The media apparently thinks that it should not be reported, or perhaps the media is controlled by the Gentiles and heathen. People are being thrown in jail for following the tenets of the Bible (James 5:12). It is nearly impossible now for one of God's people to obtain employment in industry in the United States. God condemns lawyers and judges (Luke 11:45–52). They make and interpret rules of men rather than of God, and those people who follow God are looked on with disfavor.

The United States does not have much time left. When Jesus returns to earth, all this will change. Those peoples and cities and nations who reject God's word are headed for damnation (Luke 10:10–16).

Everyone can know who God's people are by knowing those who keep God's sabbaths (Ezekiel 20:20). Saturday Sabbath keeping is an example. While God's people, the Israelites, will be persecuted, the elect will be protected (Luke 10:19).

Israelites should beware of the media people—scribes, writers, radio personnel, TV personnel, and motion picture personnel (Luke 19:47, 20:46–47). As most are controlled by and mouth the line of worldly leaders and generally ban the truths of the Bible, the Lord God warns Christians against listening to them.

As an aside, the definition of Israelite in the dictionary is not entirely correct. It proves that the Israelites have become lost in history—the ten lost tribes.

Chapter XXIII
Electronic Money Transfers

A twenty-first event leading to the destruction of the United States is the development of computers and related transfers of information and money by electronic means. Just before the end-time, the traditional ways of doing business will be done away with and an electronic money exchange system will be adopted. Money will be abolished. This is in process now in the United States. Here a little, there a little. It is being put into effect slowly so that people are unaware of the implications of it. This will first be developed and put into effect in the United States and will be adopted in the cruelest form by the new union in Europe.

In the new union in Europe, everyone who is an approved individual will be given a number and this number will be used to buy and sell and to identify a person as being in good standing, and for the purposes of taxation (extortion) control (Revelation 13:16–17). Anyone who does not have a number cannot buy and sell and cannot be anything but a beggar. This will be the method by which the powers in control of government will control the activities and affairs of all the people of the world at the end-time. The control will be by the beast (the EEC), with the advice and guidance by the great whore church at Rome and the Antichrist and the abomination of desolation, the pope (Revelation 13:1–6). It will be similar to

Fascism. Those people who do not cooperate will be persecuted. It will actually be the right thing to do to kill those who follow the Bible and Christ's teachings (Revelation 13:15). The dragon is Satan (Revelation 12:9). The ironclad control by the beast will be by means of electronic control of money transfers. When this happens, God's true disciples will not be able to participate in world commerce or affairs, because they will not be given a number. The power of the beast will be given to it by the pope and the church organization with headquarters at Rome.

This will be slavery for the masses for the benefit of those in control. The beast is the revival of the Holy Roman Empire (Revelation 13:1–6), and it will be similar to Fascism. The ruling union, called the beast, will be a powerful religious, political, military, and economic union in Europe, with Germany as the kingpin and the power, but the church at Rome will call the shots and make the decisions (Revelation 13:8). The abomination of desolation at Rome will excommunicate from the church all those who will not abide by the decisions that come from Rome. The Catholic churches will have brainwashed all their members into believing that the dogma from Rome is their only salvation. So all members will be extremely reluctant to disobey the words from Rome.

This will all come to an end when Jesus returns to earth. Those who have the mark of the beast will be destroyed (Revelation 14:9–11, 16:2, 19:20–21).

This control of the masses by a very few people at the top could not have been accomplished until the development of electronic computer technology.

Chapter XXIV
The United States Goes into Captivity

A twenty-second event that points to the end-time and destruction of the United States is that the United States will go into captivity. There is a duality all through the Bible. For example, there is a beginning Garden of Eden and there is an ending Garden of Eden, which is the present-day United States; and an Old Testament and law and a New Testament and law; a first resurrection and a second resurrection; an exodus from Egypt and an end-time exodus from heathen and Gentile countries; a destruction of earth by water and an end-time destruction by fire; a captivity in the early days by the Assyrians and an end-time captivity by the Assyrians of the Israelites, including the United States. The United States has gone into captivity just before the end of civilization as we know it (Amos 7:15–17; Ezekiel 6:1–10; Leviticus 26:31–33).

When Israel separated from Judah around 925 B.C., Israel called their center of activity Samaria. When Assyria took Israel captive about 700 B.C., they took Israel over to an area between the Caspian Sea and the Black Sea in what is now northwest Iran and southern Russia. After taking Israel captive, the Assyrians moved some of their own people into the area of Samaria. This area is now the lands north of Jerusalem. The prophecy in the Bible is that Samaria will be broken in pieces (Hosea 8:6), and in fact it is in disarray now, at this date. The Assyrians, later on the Medes, later on the Persians, and still later on the Iranians are descendants of Esau, who was Jacob's brother. Esau took a wife who was a daughter of Ishmael, who are the Arab people. Esau also took wives from the tribe of Hittites, who were black people. There was undoubtedly much intermarrying between Esau's descendants and Ishmael's descendants and also descendants of Ham and Japheth. Many of the peoples in the area of Asia Minor, Iraq, Syria, Jordan, Lebanon, and Iran would be related in a way through intermarriage.

The fact that Assyria as a national name disappeared—they were absorbed by the Medes, then later the Persians—is further evidence that the people through this area of the world are related through intermarriages.

The Israelites were commanded by God not to marry outside of their tribes, so these people remained the white people. The Israelites that were taken captive were the tribes of Ephraim, Manasseh, Dan, Reuben, Issachar, Zebulon, Naphtali, Gad, Simeon, and Asher. These are the lost ten tribes of Israel. After a few hundred years, or perhaps sooner, these tribes began to migrate north and west into Europe. In fact, at the time of Christ some had already moved into other areas.

During the period 824 to 625 B.C. the Assyrian Empire covered the territory from and including modern-day Iraq, Syria, Jordan, Lebanon, and the southern portion of modern-day Turkey southwest into and including Egypt, except the small area occupied by Judah. The Assyrian homeland covered the northern three-fourths of modern-day Iraq and Syria and the southern portion of modern-day Turkey. The Assyrians had conquered and expanded also into a portion of northwest and western modern-day Iran, so that area can be included for a part of this period of time.

Undoubtedly, many Assyrians moved north and west into Europe along with the Israelites. The Israelites are an exclusive group, mandated by God. They kept together because of God's commandments. So it is logical that the Assyrians who moved stopped along the way in Russia and eastern Europe. Many settled in eastern Germany. These people were called Aryans and were not Israelites, yet they were white people. A large part of Germany is composed of these Aryans (Assyrian people). This could very well be a mixture of Assyrian and Israelite peoples because of intermarriage. Some Israelites could have forgotten their inheritance and married non-Israelites, and as a result their children are what are called mongrels. The Israelites, who were called a peculiar people by the Gentiles and were exclusive (Exodus 19:5; Deuteronomy 14:2, 26:18; I Peter 2:9), moved on farther west and north so as to get away from the Aryans and thus be by themselves. The Aryans (Assyrians) had taken them captive, so the Israelites wanted to get away from them. The best way to do that was to move into the area of Scandinavia, the British Isles, and extreme western Europe. Many settled in western and northern Germany. The rest of Germany is mostly Aryan (Assyrian), who apparently outnumber and dominate the Israelites. This is interesting, because at the end-time Israel will go to Assyria for help out of its troubles (Hosea 8:5–9).

When the Bible speaks of Israel at the end-time, it is speaking of Ephraim (Great Britain) and the United States (Manasseh), because the inheritance of greatness was given to Abraham, then to Isaac only, then to Jacob (changed to Israel) only, then to Joseph only, then to Emphraim and Manasseh only. So when the Bible says Israel is to go to Assyria for help, it is saying that Great Britain and the United States will go to Germany, Egypt, Iran,

Syria, and Iraq for help. That is exactly what they have been doing. The other Israelite nations in Europe also look to Germany, Egypt, and Iran for strength financially and for trade in such products as oil.

Western and northern Germany is the tribe of Issachar, but the dominant group is the Aryans (Assyrians). Back through the history of Germany there have been many independent states or baronies with their individual armies, feuding with each other. The Aryans were not a cohesive unit like the Israelites. Germany is destined to be a strong ass (Hosea 8:9; Genesis 49:14–15).

In the past, the United States (Israel) has given western Germany huge sums of money through the Marshall Plan and other ways. This went to the western portion of Germany, which would be appropriate, because an Israelite nation can help another Israelite people. At the end-time, when the United States gets into financial trouble, it will go to Assyria (Germany) for help (Hosea 7, 8, 9). Thus the United States (Israel) will go into captivity by the Assyrians.

The United States has given huge sums to Egypt. Egypt at one time was taken over by the Assyrians, descendants of Esau (Hosea 9:3). The United States, at the end-time, has been begging Egypt for help in maintaining peace in the Middle East so that the oil supply lines will not be cut off. So it can be said that the United States (Israel) is captive of Egypt, also Assyrian.

The United States has also gone into captivity at the hands of the Iranians (Assyrians). The hostages that were held by the Iranians (Assyrians) were captives. The entire United States agonized over it, especially the media, and thus the entire United States was captive. As long as the media and others gave the situation so much airplay the Assyrians would continue to hold the captives and milk it for all the publicity that they can get. Israel (the United States) is captive by the Assyrians, exactly as Bible prophecy says it would be at the end-time (Ezekiel 16:53, 39:25). The Assyrians of the Middle East have been trading with Germany and there have been other associations with them, which supports the affinity between Germany and Iran and Iraq.

The Bible says that God will bring a fierce nation from afar. It will be a mighty nation, a fierce nation, an ancient nation that has a strange language that the people in Israel (the United States) do not understand (Jeremiah 5:15–17; Deuteronomy 28:47–52; Ezekiel 7). This nation is probably China or possibly Japan.

Then comes the question as to why the United States (Israel) will go into captivity. If Israel (the United States) would have followed the will of the Lord and the Ten Commandments, wonderful blessings would be received (Deuteronomy 6, 7, 8, 28:1–14). In earlier times in the United States this was done and blessings were received, but since 1950 the United States has not followed the will of God. Thus God has put a curse on the United States, because the United States (Israel) has not followed his commandments (Deuteronomy 11:26–28). He will scatter the Israelites of the United States from one end of the earth to the other (Deuteronomy 28:62–68). He will make the United States desolate (Leviticus 26:33). One-third of the Israelites of the United States will scatter to the heathen and Gentile nations of the earth, where they will be persecuted (Ezekiel 5:12–17, 6:1–14). Some will go to other Israelite nations. One-third will have died from plagues and famine, and one-third will have previously died from violence. Only the heathen and Gentiles will be left in the United States for a little while (Ezekiel 7).

The Bible says that every nation that is divided against itself will be destroyed (Mark 3:24). In the early days of the United States (Israel), only people from other Israelite nations came to the United States, those countries being Great Britain, Ireland, Norway, Sweden, Denmark, France, Belgium, Switzerland, Holland, Austria, and West Germany. Through ignorant acts of Congress and the administrations, many people from heathen and Gentile nations have been let into the United States, bringing with them different morals, ethics, religions, and pagan rituals. In accommodating their wishes and compromises made by the lawmakers in Washington, the United States has become polluted. God will see that the United States is destroyed because of that (Matthew 12:25; Luke 11:17).

The United States has lost track of its heritage and does not follow the Ten Commandments, so the United States is destroying itself (I Kings 9:6–9; Leviticus 26:27–32; Deuteronomy 8:17–20). The Israelites will flee to other nations, and many will be persecuted (Leviticus 26:33–39; Deuteronomy 7:8–10).

The leaders in Washington have spent the wealth of the United States on foolish things. There are too many to list here. That would take a book in itself. Probably the worst are the giveaways to heathen and Gentile nations, including the contributions to the World Bank, the United Nations, and the international monetary funds. These amount to gifts, as the United States gets very little in return. As a result, the United States is nearly bankrupt. The United States goes begging to Assyria (Germany, Egypt, and Iran) and seeks accommodation with Japan and other heathen and Gentile nations in order to be bailed out of its financial difficulties and trade problems (Isaiah 3:12–15; Hosea 7:8–12).

In addition to the people in Washington spending money like madmen, they have spent vast amounts of time on activities to prevent a nuclear war with the USSR. That was stupid and a complete waste of time and expense. God would not allow a nuclear war between the superpowers. Anyone who knows the Bible knows that. The war-machine makers and bankers get rich off of the preparations for war. They convinced the people and Washington officials that the USSR was out to get the United States and that we should build more tanks, more planes, and more ships than they had in the USSR. The scientists had fantastic careers devising bigger and better bombs, tanks, and planes. Because of these misguided activities, the United States is in serious trouble. God made the world (John 1:1–14), and he will not let any country or people destroy it. He will step in and see that the country or people are destroyed first. God will protect his elect (the 144,000) everywhere in the world and would not let a nuclear war destroy them. God allowed the atomic bomb to be used on Japan, because apparently there were no elect in Japan.

Now that the United States has scrapped the Monroe Doctrine, it will be just a matter of time before the heathen and Gentiles move across the borders and take over the United States. Foreigners are buying up the land, buildings, and factories of the United States and will soon dictate what goes on in the United States. Most of this purchasing is by the Arabs and Asians, who are not Israelites. Those new arrivals will soon be outvoting (with congressional mandate) the Israelites in the United States. The United States will become a banana republic. The Israelites will flee the United States.

As a result of these activities, the United States (Israel) will go into captivity (Jeremiah 10:25; Luke 21:23–24). The name Jacob in the Bible is the same as Israel. Cities of the United States (Israel) will be wasted, and houses will be without men (Isaiah 6:9–12). Many homes, even now, do not have a man in the house—single-family homes.

A remnant of Israel (12,000 from the United States and 144,000 from all tribes of Israel) will be saved and will eventually go to Jerusalem to govern the world (Isaiah 10:20–22). The remnant will come out of Assyria (Germany, where many will have fled earlier), Egypt, Pathros (southern Egypt), Cush (Ethiopia), Elam (southwest Iran), Shinar (Iraq), Hamath (north of Lebanon-Syria), and the islands of the sea (Isaiah 11:11, 15–16; Jeremiah 23:3–4). Most will come out of the north country, which will be Europe. All will be captive, just like the Israelites were in Egypt during the first captivity. This second time the captivity will be by the EEC and Assyrian peoples. All Israelite tribes will be captive (Jeremiah 23:8). The remnant of Judah will come from all nations of the earth (Isaiah 11:12). When Jesus returns, Ephraim (Great Britain) and Judah will settle their differences and the enemies of Judah will be cut off (Isaiah 11:13). Together with other Israelites, they will subdue heathen and Gentile nations (Isaiah 11:14–15). Note that Manasseh (the United States) is not mentioned because the United States will have gone into captivity and the Israelites that were in the United States will have already fled to other nations of the world and to the islands.

When Jesus returns to earth to set up his world government, the elect will be gathered together at Jerusalem. There will be 12,000 from each tribe of Israel to make up the 144,000. Included in this will be 12,000 of the Israelites originally in the United States.

The Israelites are a stiff-necked group, ambitious and opinionated. For example, only two of the men twenty years of age or older at the time of the exodus from Egypt ever saw the promised land after they came out of Egypt (Numbers 32:10–13). They failed to comprehend the significance of God's rescue of them from the land of Egypt. They thought that they knew what was good for them better than God. So God let most of them die. So today the Israelites in the United States (the white people) fail to comprehend their inheritance from God and let their own ideas of what is right and wrong dominate their thinking and thus fall into many evil ways.

At the end-time, now, in the United States you will see some of the most heinous things happen to people. Hysterical do-gooders, self-appointed authoritarian figures; power- and notoriety-hungry judges, lawyers, legislators, and bureaucrats will cause asinine programs to be adopted and people to be subjected to brutality and long prison terms. Common sense and biblical precepts will go out the window.

In retrospect, the money problems of the United States (Israel) could have been solved easily by reducing the military establishment by one-half, shipping back to where they came from all the aliens that have come into the United States in the past twenty years, and cutting off all foreign aid, including all payments to the United Nations organizations and the World Bank and international monetary funds. The trade problems could have been solved by adopting a "buy American" policy, stopping buying foreign oil, and stopping giving away American technology.

Because the United States (Israel) has failed in these matters and has forgotten its inheritance, the United States will go into captivity (Deuteronomy 27, 28, 29, 30; Ezekiel 5:6–17, 6, 7, 12:11). Just like God inspired a heathen nation, Assyria, to take Israel captive centuries ago and remove them from their homeland, Samaria, over to a desolate mountainous area and like God inspired a heathen nation, Babylon, to take Judah captive centuries ago and remove them from their homeland, Jerusalem, and scatter them to all areas of the world, so God at the end-time will inspire a heathen nation to take Israel (the United States) captive and remove them from their homeland. Because Israel (the United States) has turned its back on God's commandments and tenets, God has turned his back on the United States and allowed this to happen.

The fierce nation that destroys the United States (Israel) apparently is not the nation or nations of which Israel is captive at the end-time (Jeremiah 5:15–17; Deuteronomy 28:47–52). The nations of China and Japan are the only nations that fit all the categories stated in the Bible—Ancient Nation; Fierce Nation; Mighty Nation—and have a strange language that people of the United States (Israel) do not understand.

The Book of Ezekiel is a key book of understanding, as the prophecies in it pertain to the United States and Great Britain at the end-time.

The laws, rules, and regulations in the United States were written by lawyers. These are laws in accordance with man's interpretation of what is right and wrong rather than God's laws. God condemns lawyers and judges (Luke 11:45–52). Judges are lawyers.

Chapter XXV

Stepped-up Activity by the Abomination of Desolation

A twenty-third event occurring just before the end-time is that the pope in Rome will travel around all over the world to convert or influence all the people to Catholicism (Revelation 17). He will use the media extensively to expound his dogma and try to convert the world. He will get many nations to submit to him. His activities will cause dissension and controversy in those areas where not all have been converted to his way of thinking. This will result in killings and other troubles.

One of the biggest mistakes the United States made was when the president invited the pope to the United States. This proved that the United States had turned its back on God and made the United States, which is Israel, subject to captivity again. There is a duality all through the Bible, and this would be the end-time captivity of Israel. The captivity by the Assyrians around 800 B.C. was the first captivity of Israel. Many false prophets will emerge, doing and saying great things just before the end-time (Mark 12:38–40, 13:22; Revelation 13:11–18).

There will develop in Europe one of the greatest religious, economic, political, and military unions of all time. This union will be controlled by the Catholic Church and the pope out of Rome. The union will be a revival of the Holy Roman Empire and is called the beast in the Bible (Revelation 13:1–10). The pope at Rome and the Catholic

Church will be the power behind the beast (Revelation 13:11–18). The name will be the European Economic Community (EEC). You will note that the EEC is composed of mostly Catholic countries—France, Spain, Portugal, Italy, Greece, Luxembourg, Belgium, Germany, and Ireland. There will be two heads or control points for the EEC—one at Rome and one at Brussels or Berlin. The beast will rain fire down on earth wherever it decides to subdue and to make a point, presumably by big bomb type activity (Revelation 13:13). This ten-nation EEC will be formed just before the end-time and will last three and one-half years (Revelation 13:5). After it is formed, some of the leaders in the various united countries will shortly wake up to what is happening and will reject the pope and his organization (Revelation 17:15–18, 18). This union will rule most of the world for a very short time. It will be a time when God's people will be severely persecuted (Revelation 13:7).

Just before Jesus returns to earth to set things right, the abomination of desolation (the pope) will journey to Jerusalem (Mark 13:14–20). When you see that happen, then the end is near for the civilization as we know it. Many will head for the hills and caves at this time. A few centuries ago a prophet in Ireland prophesied as to the number of popes that there would be. According to that prophecy there will be one more pope after the current one, as of this date, January 1, 1990. When Jesus returns to earth, the pope and his system will be destroyed (Revelation 18:8–10). The pope will be killed (Deuteronomy 13:1–11; II Thessalonians 2:3–12; Revelation 18:1–2, 19:20).

While this does not pertain directly to the United States, it is included as one of the twenty-four reasons that the United States will go into captivity. Because of the Catholic Church's influence on the affairs, activities, and laws put into effect, it is an important reason for the abominable laws and decisions made by the Congress, the state legislatures, and the administrators that destroyed the United States. Many judges, senators, congressmen, legislators, and appointed officials are indoctrinated in the dogma issued from the abomination of desolation in Rome, and as a result many of the laws and regulations issued in the United States are wrong.

All the prophets and preachers who preach anything other than what is in the Bible and what Jesus taught will die (Deuteronomy 18:19–22). The threat of excommunication from the Catholic Church is overwhelming to many weak individuals who might otherwise reject some of the dogma from the abomination of desolation (Galatians 1:6–8).

Chapter XXVI

Election of a Non-Israelite as President of the United States

The twenty-fourth and final event pointing to the destruction of the United States will be the election of a person who is not an Israelite as president of the United States. God will not permit anyone who is not an Israelite to be the head of a nation of his chosen people—Israel—unless, of course, the nation has gotten so evil that God has turned his back on that nation.

The United States has always had an Israelite as president. The ancestors of all the presidents of the United States have come from Great Britain, Ireland, Holland, West Germany, Switzerland, and France. Those are all Israelite nations. In addition to those countries, the other Israelite nations are Norway, Sweden, Denmark, Luxembourg, Finland, Iceland, Belgium, Austria, and now possibly Estonia, Latvia, and Lithuania. No one whose ancestors came from any other country should ever be elected president of the United States, not if the United States wants to continue its inheritance or its existence (Deuteronomy 17:14–15).

A woman should not be elected president, because God has established roles for men and roles for women. Those people who deviate from those roles or attempt to deviate from those roles are in serious trouble (Colossians 3:18–19; I Timothy 2:9–15). A woman became head of an Israelite nation in olden times, through trickery, and death came to her because of it (II Kings 11). If a non-Israelite or a woman should become a head of government of an Israelite nation, then that would indicate that God had turned his back on the nation and that nation will decline and/or go into captivity and be in disorder.

Non-Israelites that come into an Israelite nation cannot be rulers, managers, or administrators or officers in the armed forces. If they are accepted into the nation, then they must be laborers or supervisors of laborers (I Chronicles 22:2–4; II Chronicles 2:17–18, 8:7–9).

It may happen at some time that the United States will elect a president who is not an Israelite, because the United States (Israel) is prophesied to go into captivity and Bible prophecy has never been wrong. That will mean that God has turned his back on the United States. The same can be said if a woman is ever elected president of the United States (Ezekiel 39:24–26).

The other twenty-three events stated in this book have already occurred or are in a continuing process of occurring. Thus you can see that there cannot be much time left.

Chapter XXVII
At the End-Time and After—Conclusion of the World As We Know It

A divided nation cannot stand (Luke 11:17). The United States was formed originally by Israelite people from Europe who were escaping the tyrannies of the kings and other rulers of Europe. The United States was formed for Israelites in accordance with God's covenant for Israel. The tribes of Manasseh (the United States) and Ephraim (Great Britain), sons of Joseph, received a special covenant and inheritance from Abraham, through Isaac and through Jacob, who was renamed Israel. The United States and Great Britain have enjoyed bountiful harvests, health, and wealth, and safety unknown to other nations of the world because of this inheritance.

The United States and Great Britain have now lost their inheritance because of their evil practices and wickedness (Isaiah 28:1–8; Ezekiel 11:1–12, Ezekiel 33, 36:1–20). They threw their inheritance away because they have accepted within their borders heathen and Gentiles and have accommodated them by accepting their religions, morals, and ethics and have made marriages with them. As a result, the United States and Great Britain have gone into captivity. Many Israelites living in the United States will scatter to other nations of the world (Ezekiel 12).

At the end-time, the EEC and the Roman Catholic Church will combine into the most powerful religious, political, economic, and military organization of all time. It will be a combination of Gentile and Israelite nations, dominated by the Gentile influence. Because it will resist the true God (Revelation 12), it will be called the beast (Revelation 13:12, 14:9–10). It will be a combination of Israelite nations and Gentile nations, and thus, because it is a divided union, it cannot stand. Germany is the kingpin of this organization. For a little background on the German people consider that the Israelites were taken into captivity by the Assyrians many centuries ago. Those Assyrians were later absorbed into or became the Medes, then later the Persians, and are now the Iranians. They were also known as Aryans. When the Israelites moved out of their captivity to northern and western Europe, many Assyrians (Aryans) moved or went with them. There undoubtedly was some intermarrying, despite God's commandment that Israelites must not marry with non-Israelites (Deuteronomy 7:2–3; Joshua 23:12–13). Many Assyrians (Aryans) settled in eastern Europe and Germany. Throughout the history of Germany many different groups contested with each other over territory and power. The Israelites settled mostly in western Germany and northern Germany, of those who stopped in Germany. The bulk of Germany is made up of Assyrians (Aryans). Thus when the Bible says that Israel goes to Assyria for help at the end-time, it means that the United States, Great Britain, and other Israelite nations look to Germany and other Assyrian nations for help concerning trade, including oil, and for financial help. Thus, at the end-time, the Assyrians again take captive the Israelites (the United States and Great Britain). Without Germany, the EEC would not exist. There is some business relationship among Iran, Iraq, and

Germany even at this time, so it can be said that there is an affinity between those. Also, Egypt is Assyrian (Hosea 7:11–12) and Israel goes to them for help (Hosea 9:3).

At the time that the EEC is fully operative, no one will be able to buy or sell unless he is an approved person and has a number assigned to him, such as a Social Security number. Money will be abolished. This union of European nations will control the world, including what is left of the United States. This ten-nation union, a revival of the Holy Roman Empire, will last a short time and is called the beast. During the three and one-half years when the EEC will occupy Jerusalem, God's true church and the elect will be protected (Revelation 12:14–17). After the three and one-half years, destruction comes to those people and nations that worship the beast (Revelation 14:9–11, Revelation 16). The union of European nations will finally wake up to what has been happening and will turn on the whore, which is the church at Rome, and make her desolate (Revelation 17).

After the United States goes into captivity, the dominant group of nations will be the EEC. A key area to watch at this time will be Jerusalem. From out of the north an army will come down into western Asia and take over the area and restore order (Luke 21:20–21, Jeremiah 49:39, 50:3). Babylon will be taken—Iraq, Syria, Lebanon, Jordan, Elam, and western Iran—and the nation that calls itself Israel at this time (Jeremiah 50:1–16). This army from the north is undoubtedly from NATO, which is also the EEC. The United States will already be captive to that organization, as well as a part of it. The Holy City, Jerusalem, will be occupied by Gentiles from the north for three and one-half years (Revelation 11:2). This means that the nation that calls itself Israel today will be controlled for three and one-half years. This will be done by the European military, political, religious, and economic power, the EEC. It will be a revival of the Holy Roman Empire, and the pope will actually rule over it. The pope will travel to Jerusalem and actually set up headquarters there (Revelation 13:4–5; Mark 13:14; Matthew 24:15–20). The EEC will be considered Gentile because of the pope's rule and because Italy, Spain, Greece, Portugal, and much of Germany cannot be considered Israelite territory. The Israelite nations in western Europe—France, Belgium, the Netherlands, Denmark, Luxembourg, Ireland, and Great Britain—will be captive to the ruling authorities of the EEC, dominated by Germany. Most of those nations are Catholic nations. It is possible that Denmark and Great Britain will pull out of the union because of religious differences and other reasons. There are twelve nations in the union now, so two will pull out at some time.

When Jerusalem becomes surrounded by armies from the north, the end will come (Luke 21:20–21), after three and one-half years. Then the great tribulation will come at this time (Revelation 7:1–3, Revelation 8). The army from the north will be the armies of NATO (EEC) rather than from the USSR, because the pope will be involved in the occupation (Matthew 24:15–22).

Times will be so bad at this time that men will eat men (Ezekiel 5:9–10). All nations and people that will not obey God's commandments will be destroyed (Isaiah 34:1–10, 54:15, 60:12; II Thessalonians 1:8–9). The United States will be desolate (Ezekiel 6).

Shortly thereafter, Jesus will return to earth to set up his ruling kingdom for earth and to destroy the wicked peoples (Matthew 13:49–50; I Corinthians 15:24–25). The pope will be destroyed (Revelation 19:18–21; II Thessalonians 2:3–12). God made the universe through the Word, who is Jesus, and Jesus will be heir to all things. Jesus looks like God (Hebrews 1:1–3). A remnant of Israel and Judah will be saved (Romans 9:27). The remnant will come from Europe, land of the north, the area around Asia Minor, and from the islands, to Jerusalem to establish the world ruling headquarters with Jesus (Isaiah 11:11–12; Hosea 1:10–11; Jeremiah 3:14–19). This remnant will be the 144,000, which will be composed of 12,000 from each of the twelve tribes of Israel, except the tribe of Dan (Revelation 7:4–8). With the tribe of Joseph split into two tribes—Ephraim and Manasseh—it makes thirteen tribes; however, the tribe of Dan is excluded, so it reverts back to twelve tribes. This new nation at Jerusalem will be called Israel (Ezekiel 37:16–28), and it will be very different from the nation that calls itself Israel today. The 144,000 are identified in the Bible (Revelation 14:1–5; Luke 20:34–36). The twelve apostles will be resurrected and will sit on thrones in Jerusalem, judging the twelve tribes of Israel (Luke 22:30; Matthew 19:28, 23:39).

With regards to the dead, when Jesus returns to earth the elect will be resurrected and brought to Jerusalem. The rest of the dead will not be resurrected until a thousand years are completed (Revelation 20:4–7) and the judgment (Revelation 20:12–15; II Corinthians 5:10). Of the Israelites from the United States, many have scattered to all nations and been persecuted there (Deuteronomy 4:25–31). Some will survive the tribulation and be rescued when Jesus returns to earth (Isaiah 11:12, 27:12–13; Jeremiah 16:15–16; Revelation 7:9–17; Jeremiah 50:18–20; Deuteronomy 4:25–31; Ezekiel 36:16–38, 37:1–14, 15–28). God will put a curse on all those who hated the Israelites (Deuteronomy 30:1–8; Ezekiel 28:25–26). Also, many Gentile people, and possibly many who had no religious teaching prior to the tribulation and who survived the tribulation, will come before Jesus and, if they follow God's commandments over a period of time, will receive salvation. The righteous and wicked will be judged (Ecclesiastes 3:17; Revelation 20:12–13). Strangers who have not followed God's commandments and tenets of the Bible shall not enter into God's Kingdom (Ezekiel 44:6–9). Israelites must put away its whoredoms and abominations in order to enter into God's Kingdom (Ezekiel 43:7–12).

The world headquarters will be established at a new Jerusalem by Jesus and his 144,000 elect (Revelation 3:12, 21:2), and worldwide rule will be from there to all nations (Revelation 20:4). During the 1,000 years' rule peace will be with all nations, and the nations that do not obey will be destroyed (Isaiah 2:2–5). There cannot be any peace now among nations until Jesus returns to rule.

The elect (the 144,000) will enjoy many beautiful things (Isaiah 4:2). Those that follow Jesus and the Ten Commandments will be saved (Romans 10). Many people who have followed other religions, other than what Jesus proclaimed, and think that they are saved may be in for a rude awakening. The wisdom of the world is foolishness with God (I Corinthians 3:18–19). Those who have the faith and follow God's commandments can become children of Abraham and be saved, even if they are not Israelites (Galatians 3:6–29; Ephesians 3:6; Romans 9:24–26, 33).

The United States will have gone into captivity previous to the tribulation. The elect will have been sealed from harm and taken to places of protection (Revelation 12:13–17). Some areas of the earth will be destroyed by fire (Isaiah 26:11, 66:15–16; Revelation 9:18). Some people will survive the tribulation (Isaiah 24:1–6). The moon and sun will be strange during the tribulation (Isaiah 24:19–23; Revelation 8:7–13). Just before Jesus returns, the sun will darken and the moon will give no light (Mark 13:24–25). Fire will destroy the wicked. The enemies of Israel will be destroyed completely (Luke 19:27; Micah 5:9; Psalms 92:9). After the tribulation, a new world will be established with headquarters at Jerusalem (Isaiah 65:17–25, 66:15–24). After 1,000 years, the dead will be resurrected and no longer will anyone be buried in the ground (Isaiah 26:19–21).

There will be great destruction of peoples and nations during the tribulation (Jeremiah 25:32–33; Ezekiel 9) where the Israelites have been captive (Jeremiah 30:10–16), but Israelites who follow God's word will be protected. A remnant of Israel, not the 144,000, who have survived the tribulation will journey to Jerusalem for instruction in the way of the Lord (Jeremiah 31:6–12, 50:17–19; Matthew 24:21–31).

Over the years there has been much speculation concerning Armageddon or, in some cases, the "battle of Armageddon." This will actually not be much of a battle. The people and troops from the north, the EEC, who have established order in the western Asia area—Iraq, Syria, Jordan, Lebanon, western Iran, parts of Arabia, and the nation that calls itself Israel today—will be destroyed after their three and one-half years' occupation. Those troops will have come down from the north, which would be from NATO or the EEC (Jeremiah 50–51; Revelation 16). With God's intervention, the troops who had occupied this area will simply die, perhaps by fire or perhaps simply by dropping dead. At this time also Assyria (Iran, Iraq, Jordan, Syria, Lebanon, and Egypt) will be destroyed (Micah 4–5; Zechariah 10:11; Zephaniah 2:12–13; II Samuel 22:38–43). At this same time the abomination of desolation (the pope) will be destroyed (Revelation 17, 19:18–21; Luke 12:49).

At the end-time, mountains and islands will disappear (Revelation 6:14; Isaiah 40:4, 54:10) or move out of their places. There will be a complete arrangement of the earth's features. The environmentalists have very little knowledge of what is in the Bible, or they would know that their complaints, sit-ins, etc., are a complete waste of time and money. The programs of NASA, space exploration, Star Wars, and "Supercollider" are a complete waste of time and money. Those who are working on those projects can never know what goes on in the universe or how it was created. What do they think they will do with the information that they find? Do they plan to destroy the universe and build a new universe? The wisdom of the world is foolishness (I Corinthians 3:19). Much time and money is spent on determining what UFOs are. Spirit beings can move with the speed of lightning. When humans are resurrected, they are resurrected as spirit beings just as Jesus was resurrected. They can make themselves visible or invisible. Heat and cold do not affect them. Movement can be instantaneous, if they want it that way (John 3:8). The Lord controls the angels or spirit beings, who can destroy nations and peoples (II Samuel 24:15–16; Matthew 17:3, Matthew 13, 24:27).

After the tribulation, God's elect will assemble at Jerusalem with Jesus to establish the new nation of Israel and the world headquarters. After the destruction of the EEC and Assyrians and the return of Jesus, there will be a 1,000-year period when the people left on the earth will receive instruction in the tenets of the Bible for purposes of receiving salvation. Many of these people will have had no knowledge of Jesus Christ, what Jesus said, or the tenets of the Bible (Revelation 15:4).

There will be no more sea when Jesus establishes his new world order (Revelation 21:1). There will not be a sun or moon shining on Jerusalem (Revelation 21:23–24). It will be light all the time (Isaiah 60:19–20). At the end-time, men will hide themselves in caves (Revelation 6:15), but it will do them no good.

Jerusalem has been reduced to ashes seventeen times and has risen out of those ashes each time. There have been thirty-six wars around Jerusalem, according to information from the Israel Government Tourist Office, Embassy of Israel, Washington, D.C. Wars and turmoil will all end when Jesus comes back to earth and the elect from the twelve tribes of Israel assemble at Jerusalem and with Jesus rule the world from there (Ezekiel 20:33). It will be the permanent world headquarters unto eternity. Those people who think that they will go to heaven will be surprised to know that heaven is here on earth, after Jesus returns (Genesis 1:6–8).

The holy area for the home of God's people was established by God a long time ago. Please refer to Genesis 28:10–22. Bethel is very close to Jerusalem, so the whole area around Jerusalem is considered holy land and is to be the home of Israel, God's people. God has allowed some heathen and Gentile people to occupy the area on occasion when the Israelites did bad things and were banished from the area. The Israelites are a group (perhaps even race) of select people, so no stranger can become an Israelite. However, it is possible for a stranger to become one of Abraham's seed and saved if he follows God's commandments (Galatians 3:29). Israel is God's people (Ezekiel 34:30–33), and King David and his seed have God's mercy forever (II Samuel 22:51).

This is revealing concerning the proliferation of atomic weapons knowledge and atomic weapons by various countries. The ability for the world to destroy itself by fire is an accomplished fact. It is another proof that civilization as we know it is about to end. God says in the Bible that the world would finally get so evil that it will have to be destroyed a second time, not by water, but by fire. The elect will be saved (Revelation 14:1–5; Isaiah 66:15–16; Ezekiel 20:43–48).

Liberated women of ease will be in serious trouble (Isaiah 32:9–14). Eunuchs will be given an everlasting name and a good place in the world of the new order (Isaiah 56:3–5; Revelation 14:1–5). This may shock some of the worldly thinkers of modern times. Those that are of God hear God's word (John 8:47), and those that are not of God cannot hear God's word. God closes the ears of those that are not of God or at least does not give them understanding. That is why there is so much crime, war, and other bad things today. People are doing what men think is right instead of what God says is right, as stated in many, many places in the Bible. The old world of Noah's time was destroyed by water for its evil ways. Today's world will be reserved for judgment by fire (II Peter 3:5–7, 10–13).

At the end of the 1,000 years of peace, Satan will be released from his chains to again roam the earth for a short time. Satan will stir up Gog, Magog, Gomer, Togarmah, Mesheck, Tubal, Persia, Ethiopia, Libya, Sheba, Dedan, and Tarshish to battle against the Saints. Those peoples are the former USSR, except the Baltic states, Eastern Europe, Armenia, Georgia, Asia, Azerbaijan, Turkey, Libya, Ethiopia, Saudi Arabia, Qatar, the United Arab Emirates, and the islands off Asia and southern Europe. These peoples will be destroyed (Ezekiel 38, 39; Zephaniah 2:11–12; Revelation 20:7–9).

The Bible, or the understanding of the Bible, has been closed to all but a very few elect, because of God's purpose for earth. At the end-time, knowledge is revealed (Daniel 12:9) because God's purpose, for the first 6,000 years of existence of man is done and there is no more reason to keep it a secret. This book is a revelation of knowledge for all who can read (Isaiah 29:10–24). A watchman is to warn Israel of the word of the Lord (Ezekiel 33:2–29, 30–33).

God's purpose for earth for the first 6,000 years is to let people develop their character and personality, preferably in God's image. But it is up to each individual. That is so God can know who he can trust to govern with him in his new world. Before the time of man, creating spirit beings or angels didn't work very well, because many of these, including Satan, the chief among them, defected and turned against God. Those humans who do not meet God's standards will be destroyed (Amos 9:10).

God created earth in six days and then rested on the seventh day. A day is a thousand years according to God's way of counting time (II Peter 3:8). This same seven-day period or, rather, a like seven-day period is allotted to man to develop his character in God's image. Six days (6,000 years) is allotted to man on his own, plus another day (1,000 years) after Jesus returns to earth to supervise the affairs of man (Genesis 1–2). God knew that man on his own could not learn the ways of peace and health but instead could only know suffering and death. So God provided a seventh day (1,000 years) after Jesus returns for man to learn peace and good health.

This same seven-day period is also mandated for our human existence on man's way of counting time. Thus six days—Sunday through Friday—are man's days to do what he thinks best, and a seventh (Saturday) day, the last day of the week, is mandated for a day of rest for man (Exodus 23:12, 31:15).

False prophets and Sunday preachers, over the years, talking about Christ but not what Christ said to do will perish (II Corinthians 11:13–15; Matthew 12:34, 15:7–9, 23:33, 24:11). Satan (the devil) has power over the world today until Jesus returns (Luke 4:5–7). Those who do not reject Satan's power are lost.

Salvation is of the Jews (John 4:22). This is because Jesus and the apostles were Jews, as were the writers of the Bible, except Luke. The Jews were to keep the oracles of God. Those who refuse to hear the words of God are condemned (Matthew 10:14–15; Mark 8:37–38).

For those who want to know what God looks like, refer to Revelation 1:14–15. Humans are made in God's image (Genesis 1:26–27). In other words, we humans look like God. Jesus was a plain-looking man, of medium height or less, unrecognized in a crowd (Luke 4:28–30). Those who receive Jesus receive God (Mark 9:37).

The end of civilization as we know it will come quickly, suddenly, without warning (Mark 13:4–37; Luke 21:7–36).

Those people that are saved will be taken up into the clouds around earth and whisked like an eagle to Jerusalem (Luke 17:34–37). Those people who will not accept Christ will be destroyed (Luke 19:27). Those people who think that the law—the commandments and tenets of the Bible—has been done away with are seriously mistaken. The commandments and tenets of the Bible are firm for all time (Luke 16:17).

Epilogue

When one contemplates all the things that have happened to the United States in the last forty years and the destruction of the United States, the greatest nation on earth, one wonders how it could possibly have happened. Have the leaders in Washington that let this happen been so evil or ignorant, or were they just putting into effect the policies that the people wanted? It would not now be possible to throw out or cancel out all the policies and undo all the actions that they have put into effect in the last forty years. It would be an enormous undertaking to undo or reverse all the bad laws and regulations that destroyed Israel (United States), which Congress, state legislatures, and administrations have put into effect. Also, the morals of the people of the United States would have to be completely turned around to the right way.

The prophecies of the Bible have always come true, so the fate of the United States is fixed. The only question is just when. The United States as a nation will not be able to change enough to prevent its destiny. In the early days of the United States, the Israelites dominated the government affairs. They thought alike and government worked smoothly, comparatively speaking. In the later days of this century, the wrangling in government has made it impossible to govern the nation like the Bible says it should be governed. Heathen and Gentiles have been let into the United States, and some of their thinking and customs have been adopted. Thus the United States has become a stench in the nostrils of God. There is an old saying "Put one rotten apple in a barrel of apples, and very soon the entire barrel of apples will be rotten." Worldly people and their projects will be destroyed (I John 3:8; Genesis 11:1–9).

The whole arena in the United States is upside down. Heathen have preference in hiring, schooling, grants, voting, recreation, and TV and other media coverage. The lame and lazy have preference in the best parking areas, seating areas, food, and medical care (Exodus 23:3).

Following are listed the presidents during whose administrations Israel (the United States) as a nation disintegrated:

1. Abraham Lincoln—during this period the destruction of the United States began. The turmoil and unnecessary deaths and hatreds that occurred during this period, and which are still with the United States today, cracked open the foundation on which the United States was built.
2. Franklin Roosevelt—during this period the United States adopted policies and laws that would result in eventually bankrupting the United States. Roosevelt wouldn't allow the freeing of eastern Europe and became partners with the heathen in dismantling Europe, resulting in the deaths of many freedom-loving people. The Yalta affair was an abomination.
3. Harry Truman—the Korean debacle was the firm evidence that the United States had become a wimp and a coward, after starting the war and then not completing the job. Also during this period, earth-shaking rules and regulations were put into effect that destroyed the Israelites' ability to function in a manner that God commanded.

4. John Kennedy—during this period the United States abandoned the Monroe Doctrine and allowed the heathen to get a foothold in the Americas and in Congress and the legislative halls of America. JFK started the Vietnam involvement and the cooperation with the EEC.
5. Lyndon Johnson—during this period the inner strength that made the United States great was ripped up and thrown out. The heathen and Gentiles took control of the United States.

Another indication that the end-time is very near is the fact that in many nations women are being put in charge of government. In addition to those mentioned in chapter 4, you can add Iceland, Norway, Nicaragua, Ireland, Bangladesh, and the Dominican Republic. Those countries will deteriorate and have all kind of problems.

Ezekiel was commissioned to speak to the house of Israel (the lost ten tribes). He couldn't at the time he was living, because he was a slave captive with the tribe of Judah in Babylon. The message in the Book of Ezekiel is for Israel (the United States and Great Britain) today (Ezekiel 3:1–4). Israel was appointed to a new place to live other than the area around Jerusalem (II Samuel 7:10). This new place to live was in the sea north and west of Jerusalem, which could only mean the British Isles (Genesis 28:14; Isaiah 41:1, 43:5–6, 49:1–3, 12, 51:5; Jeremiah 3:18, 31:7–10; I Chronicles 17:9). The throne of David is established forever in the British Isles until the time of the end, when it will move to Jerusalem (II Samuel 7:11–29). David's throne was overturned when all the male heirs in David's line were killed by the Babylonians. Jeremiah took the throne with him when he escaped to Ireland. A surviving daughter of King Zedekiah in David's line accompanied Jeremiah to Ireland. Her name was Tea-Tephi and she had previously married a son of King Herremon of Ireland, who was Hebrew royalty of the line of Zerah and had moved to Ireland much earlier. Thus from this daughter, Tea-Tephi, a part of David continues on to this day in the succession to David's throne. The throne was overturned first to Ireland, then to Scotland, and then overturned again when it moved to England (Ezekiel 17, 21:26–27). (See also exhibit 5.) When the throne of David moves to Jerusalem, Jesus Christ will take it over (Luke 1:32; Ezekiel 21:25–27).

Ireland is the tribe of Dan. However, some from the tribe of Judah also went to Ireland, at least for a while. Some went with Jeremiah when he escaped to Ireland, and some went earlier. The people of Ireland have elected a woman as their president, so it appears that God has turned his back on Ireland. This is confirmed in the Bible, as the tribe of Dan is excluded from the elect who will rule from the new headquarters at Jerusalem.

The people of Judah (the tribes of Judah, Benjamin, and Levi) were scattered to all the nations of the world. There will be 12,000 from each of those tribes in the elect that will rule the world with Jesus, so there will be a total of 36,000 who are now called Jews that will return to their original name of Israel, along with the other nine tribes, when Jesus sets up his new government. There are many Jews who are "jumping the gun," as it were, and returning to Jerusalem now. However, these Jews who are returning now will suffer many troubles in the next few years. I believe that many of the 36,000 are even now scattered in many countries of the world and will remain in those places up until the time of the end and Jesus' return. Then they will assemble at Jerusalem along with the elect from each of the other tribes of Israel.

The reason God changed the name Israel to Britain and America was because the name Israel and also Jew became dirty words or curses to the inhabitants of the world (Jeremiah 29:18, 44:8; Daniel 9:11; Lamentations 3:65; Zechariah 8:13; Isaiah 65:15). God did not want his chosen people to be burdened with negative opinions by other world peoples, so he changed their name. In addition to a new name for his chosen people, God also gave them a new language—English. Thus his chosen people became lost in history.

As for the Jews (Judah, Benjamin, and Levi) who were banished to all areas of the world because of their abominations, at the end-time those Jews that have followed the commandments of the Bible will probably be forgiven when Jesus Christ returns to earth the second time.

The name Israel will be restored to the twelve tribes, and the new nation at Jerusalem will be called Israel. The new nation of Israel will be considerably different from the nation that calls itself Israel today. It will combine Judah and Israel (Ezekiel 37:21–22).

A key to understanding is that ten tribes of Israel separated from the other tribes a long time ago (II Samuel 19:41–43, 20:1–2). The ten tribes are Israel, while Judah, Benjamin, and Levi are Judah (the Jews). Also, the dragon is Satan, the beast is the Holy Roman Empire (the EEC), and the false prophet is the pope (Revelation 16:13–14).

Many people wonder why so many people of the Middle East hate the Jews in the nation that calls itself Israel today. The answer to that is in Genesis 27. The descendants of Esau are the Assyrians. These people are located now in Iran, northern Iraq, Jordan, Lebanon, Syria, southern Turkey, and Egypt. These people are not the Arabs, who are descendants of Ishmael. (Because of intermarriage and mixing in this area there are some Arabs who hate the

Jews, but generally this is not true.) So there can never be peace in the Middle East between the Assyrians and the Jews. Esau vowed to kill Jacob (Israel) over the birthright issue.

There can be no peace in the world now because of Satan's influence in stirring up greed, lust, and power grabbing in those he can convert to evil practices. As a result God has to stir up his chosen people (Israel) and nation to go to war to destroy the despots and tyrants.

The throne of David is established forever, and it is to be over Israel forever (I Kings 2:45, 8:16). It has been in the British Isles ever since Jeremiah escaped from Jerusalem with the throne. The Lord will grant peace forever for David's throne, house, and seed (I Kings 2:33). There will always be a man in David's line sitting on Israel's throne (David's throne) unless the people of Israel fail to follow God's commandments and tenets. Because the people of Israel have failed with regards to this, a woman has been allowed to sit on David's throne near the end-time (I Kings 8:25). A woman on David's throne would still have to be in David's line.

There is some talk now of a "new world order." A new world order based on greed, lust, and power would be an abomination. All rights of individuals would be abolished, and everyone would live at a poverty level except those in power. Dreamers who picture an utopian world have no idea what is in the Bible or how humans think. Those people who are promoting a new world order know very little about human nature and history of the Bible and of the world and the commandments and tenets of the Bible. Ethnic groups have always disagreed with each other and fought against each other. Even in the churches there is disagreement and fighting when there should be harmony. The fact that Israelites have enjoyed health, wealth, safety, prosperity, and bountiful harvests was no accident. It was God-decreed. All you have to do is compare Africa, Asia, South America, and Central America to the Israelite nations to see the difference. Those people who want to uplift the poverty in third world countries to the prosperity of the United States are completely wrong. There is no way that the people and nations in non-Israelite areas can be lifted up to compare with the Israelite nations.

There will be a new world order very soon, established by Jesus Christ when he returns to earth. Those people who qualify to live in the new world will never know poverty and sickness (Revelation 7:14–17; Luke 18:30).

I told you in a previous chapter that there is a duality all through the Bible and history. At the beginning of civilization in the Garden of Eden, it was Eve, through her lusts for goodies and lust for dominance over those around her, who destroyed the perfect Garden of Eden, which God had created for mankind. So again, at the end-time, in the end-time Garden of Eden (the United States), the Eves of the United States have, through their votes, laws giving preference in hiring, and other manipulations, destroyed the end-time Garden of Eden. God is in control of the universe, and he will destroy the end-time Garden of Eden, just like he did the first Garden of Eden. Just as Eve through her wiles got Adam to turn away from God, so now the modern-day Eves through their wiles are causing their men to turn away from God.

God is the God of Abraham, Isaac, and Jacob (Israel) (Matthew 22:32). Jesus did not do away with the Ten Commandments (Matthew 22:36–40, 5:17–22, 19:17–19), and those people who follow the Ten Commandments can have their prayers answered (Matthew 21:21–22). False prophets, teachers, and preachers will be in serious trouble (II Peter 2:1). Preachers are not to be called Rabbi or Father or make long prayers (Matthew 23:2–15).

From Adam to Noah there were only three people whom God approved—Abel, Enoch, and Noah (Genesis 4:4, Genesis 5). After Noah there have been many others to make up the 144,000 elect. The true apostles (the twelve) were apparently fairly successful in getting the Israelites to change their ways. Those people whom God approves will be resurrected as angels or, in other words, spirit beings (Matthew 19:29, 22:30). The Holy Ghost is the Holy Spirit that enters into a person when he accepts God's way of living (Mark 1:8, 12:25; Matthew 28:19).

Jesus came to earth the first time because the people on earth, including his chosen people, had gotten so evil that God would have to destroy the people again if they didn't change their ways. Jesus and his apostles did get many people to change their ways. At the present time people have gotten so evil that God will have to destroy the people on earth again, except for his elect.

At the end-time, when God turns his back on Israel (the United States), a fierce nation will rise up to destroy Israel (the United States). That will signal the end of civilization as we know it, the destruction of peoples, and the return of Jesus Christ. The tribulation will be terrible (Revelation 8, 9; Ezekiel 5, 6, 7).

This book was all ready to be sent in for publishing in the first part of August 1990. However, because of the police action by the United States and the coalition in the Arabian Peninsula against Iraq, it was withheld at that time.

There is great euphoria in the United States concerning the police action in the Arabian Peninsula; however, it really didn't accomplish much. It left the area in disarray and disorder and a shambles. There will be much killing in the area. The police action really didn't settle anything, and the United States really didn't win anything. An Israelite nation, if it is stirred up by God to go to war against a people, should destroy everything that made the offending nation bad and lay waste to the nation. The police action did not accomplish that and thus was a failure. This is the same as happened in Korea and Vietnam.

The United States is trying to be a friend of the world. A friend of the world cannot enter into God's Kingdom (James 4:4; Luke 7:34, 9:25). Offering money or other compensation or favors to other members of the coalition to go along with the strategy concerning the operation of the police action was an abomination. It was buying lovers, and everyone knows what that is. If the United States goes into Iraq to rebuild it, it will be an abomination.

The United States is finished as a great nation. It will become like a third-world country or a banana republic. It will lose its inheritance of bountiful harvests, good health, wealth, prosperity, and safety from its enemies, unless it can change radically and quickly.

Twenty-three of the twenty-four matters leading to the destruction of the United States (Israel) have already occurred or have already started and are in process of accelerating to completion. The only item left yet to occur is that item described in chapter 26. It is the final nail in the coffin of the United States.

The Bible is God's handbook for people to use as a guide for living according to his commanded way of life, in order to have eternal life. If one follows the commandments and tenets of the Bible right down the line, no one can hurt him and his prayers will be answered, unless he prays for something that is amiss or is not in accordance with the natural laws under which the universe operates. For example, all flesh has to die sometime, so one can't pray to keep someone alive forever. One can't deliberately jump off a ten-story building and not get killed when he hits the ground.

Jesus Christ was an ordinary, plain-looking man of average height or less for a Jew of that time. He was not distinguished from anyone else (Luke 24:15–18). The Jews of that day had Jesus killed. The Roman authorities did not want to kill Jesus but wanted to turn him free. However, the Jews insisted that he be killed (Luke 23). The Romans were Gentiles (Luke 23:16, 20). Because the people on earth had gotten so evil that God would have to destroy everyone on it if people didn't change, God sent his son, Jesus Christ, to earth to convert people to God's way and thus save the world (John 3:15–18). So now, the world has again gotten so evil that God will have to destroy it unless people can be converted to God's way of living. Thus Jesus Christ will soon be sent by God to earth again so the world can be saved.

Jesus Christ arose from the dead and walked, talked, and ate with his disciples and others. Jesus could disappear and reappear at will (Luke 24:15–51). Jesus ate meat with his disciples, after the resurrection. Those people who are resurrected at the second coming of Jesus Christ can do the same. Also, those who are resurrected later, after the 1,000 years (John 3:8).

The universe was made by the Word (John 1:1–5), and the Word is Jesus Christ (John 1:14). Jesus Christ is the son of God (John 1:18).

There are some mercenaries, social engineers, media personnel, and those ignorant of God's word and plan for earth who are trying to force the integration of people of different ethnic groups and racial backgrounds. Those who try to countermand God's plan for earth cannot be accepted into God's Kingdom. Only those who obey God can be accepted into God's Kingdom (Matthew 4:4; Luke 11:28; John 5:24, 38, 14:24; Acts 5:32, 13:26; I Peter 1:23, 4:17; II Peter 1:10–11; Hebrews 5:9; II Thessalonians 1:5–8, 3:14; Galatians 1:5–8).

It is interesting that our leaders are pushing for democracy for all nations and all peoples of the world, including one vote for each individual to determine the laws, rules, and regulations for all people's lives. When Jesus Christ returns to earth soon, it will be a strict dictatorship and rule by one person—Jesus Christ as God—establishing all the laws, rules, and regulations for the lives of all people on earth. Those people who do not comply with those laws, rules, and regulations will simply drop dead (Revelation 20:8–9).

Those that are friends of the world and world affairs are enemies of God (James 4:4). God does not change. The commandments and tenets of the Bible are for all time (Malachi 3:6; Hebrews 13:8; John 5:46).

The United States has been the greatest nation of all time. It is the end-time Garden of Eden. I think that everyone in the world will acknowledge that. No one should want to hurt the United States. Yet the greed and lust for money, power, and pleasures by many individuals has resulted in the pollution and destruction of the United States. If the United States (Israel) cannot change quickly and completely, then the United States will become like a third-world nation or a banana republic and Israelites will begin to leave in droves (Ezekiel 4:13, 5:12, 6, 7). However, it is possible that the United States could go the way of Sodom and Gomorrah (Genesis 18:20–33, 19:1–28; Jude 7).

Because God has turned his back on the United States, no program that our elected officials try to put into effect for such things as education, environment, health, welfare, housing, safety, transportation, crime control, AIDS, foreign policy, etc., will be a success. They will all be a disaster. The officials will throw money at the programs, but it will be a waste of money as well as energy and time. Make no mistake about it—God does not give his blessings to any people or nation that does not follow his commandments and tenets as stated in the Bible.

Because this book is published you will know that civilization as we know it is nearing the end (Daniel 12:4–9; Ezekiel 7, 33:2–20, 30–33). The people of the United States (Israel) have been warned, as have all Israelites (Ezekiel 33; Acts 3:20–26). It is up to each individual as to which way he will go. Each will give an accounting to God (Romans 14:8–13; John 5:28–29).

This book reveals the information that has been closed up until the time-of-the-end.

Exhibits

Exhibit I
Writers of the Bible

The following is a listing of who wrote the Bible or are the words of:

Book of the Bible	Words of or Written By
Genesis, Exodus, Leviticus, Numbers, and Deuteronomy	Moses
Joshua	Joshua
Judges and I Samuel from 1 to 24	Samuel
I Samuel 25–31 and II Samuel	Nathan and Gad
Ruth	Samuel
I Kings and II Kings	Jeremiah
I Chronicles and II Chronicles	Ezra
Ezra, Nehemiah, Job, Daniel, Isaiah, Jeremiah, Ezekiel, Hosea, Joel, Amos, Obadiah, Jonah, Micah, Nahum, Habakkuk, Zephaniah, Haggai, Zechariah, Solomon, Malachi	All these were written by themselves
Esther	Unknown
Ecclesiastes	Solomon
Lamentations	Jeremiah
Psalms	David, Asaph, and Moses
Proverbs	Soloman, Agur, and Lemuel
Matthew, Mark, Luke, John, James, Jude, Peter I and II, John I and II and III	All these were written by themselves
The Acts	Luke
Romans, I Corinthians, II Corinthians,	Paul

Galatians, Ephesians, Philippians, Colossians, I Thessalonians, II Thessalonians, I Timothy, II Timothy, Titus, Philemon, and Hebrews	
Revelation	John

Exhibit II
Genealogy

Noah had three sons, Shem, Ham, and Japheth, whose descendants are as follows:

Sons of Shem—the white people (I Chronicles 1,2,3) Genesis 10:21-32):

- Elam
- Asshur
- Lud
- Aram—Uz, Hul, Gether, Mash, and Meshech
- Arphaxad—Shelah (Salah), Eber, Peleg, Joktan, and then several others to Abram (changed to Abraham)
  - The descendants of Abram led to the Israelites through his son Isaac and Isaac's son Jacob (name changed to Israel).
  - Also, Abraham had a second wife, Keturah, who had sons:
    - Zimran
    - Jokshan—Sheba and Dedan—Asshurim, Letushim, and Leummim
    - Medan
    - Midian—Ephah, Epher, Hanoch, Abida, and Eldaah
    - Ishbak
    - Shuah
    - (Genesis 25:1–6; Exodus 2:16–22, 3:1)
  - Other descendants were Dedan, Sheba, Ophir, Havilah, Uzal, and Hazarmaveth.

Sons of Ham—the black people (I Chronicles 1; Genesis 10:6–20):

Cush—Nimrod (Babylon), Seba, Havilah, Sabtah (Sabta), Raamah, Sheba, Dedan, and Sebtecha
Phut (Put)
Mizraim—Ludim, Anamim, Lehabim, Naphtuhim, Pathrusim, Caphtorim, and Caaluhim (the Philistines)
Canaan—Zidon, Heth—also tribes of Jebusites, Amorite, Girgashite, Hivite, Arkite, Sinite, Arvadite, Zemarite, and Hamathite

Sons of Japheth—the brown, yellow, and red people (I Chronicles 1; Genesis 10:2–5):

Gomer—Ashchenaz, Riphath, and Togarmah
Magog, also Gog
Madai
Javan—Tarshish (in Spain, Portugal, and islands), Elishah, Kittim, and Dodanim
Tubal
Meshech
Tiras

Exhibit III

Where Jesus' Disciples (Apostles) Went

The Disciples went to the various areas as follows:

Simon Peter—went to the western Mediterranean (Spain) and then to the British Isles.
Some of the Israelites migrated first to Spain and then moved on to Ireland and Britain.

Andrew—went to the area north of the Black Sea (Scythia), to the south shore of the Black Sea, to Crimea, and to the Caucasus Mountain area.
The Anglo-Saxons and Scots came from Scythia.

James, son of Alphaeus—went to Spain, where the Israelites stopped temporarily, then to Ireland, then to Britain.

Simon—went to North Africa, Libya and Egypt, then to Ireland, then to Britain.
Some Saxons came through Africa to Spain and then to Britain.

Thomas—went to Parthia, which is south of the Caspian Sea, in present-day Iran, then to western India and to Afghanistan.

The Israelites in western India were called White Indians.
These all migrated later to northwestern Europe, probably North Germany, the Frisian Islands, and Baltic Region.

Bartholomew—went to upper Asia Minor (now Turkey), to Armenia, and to Parthia south of the Caspian Sea.

Jude*—went to Assyria, to Mesopotamia (modern Iraq), and to Parthia south of the Caspian Sea (now Iran).

Phillip—went to Scythia north of the Black and Caspian Seas (the modern-day Ukraine) and to northern Asia Minor.
The Scots came from that area.

Matthias—went to western Scythia and to modern-day Romanian and Macedonian areas.
The Normans who later settled Scandinavia, France, and Britain came from there.

Matthew—went to the Caspian Sea area, to Parthia (modern Iran), and to western India and Hindu Kush (modern Afghanistan).
These Israelites later migrated to northwestern Europe.

John—went to Gaul (now France).
The care of Mary, mother of Jesus, was assigned to John.

James, John's brother—was beheaded by Herod.

---

*Also known as Judas, the brother of James.

This information was taken from an article 1964, 1973 issued by the Worldwide Church of God, Pasadena, California. This is from an eight-page publication titled "Where Did the Twelve Apostles Go?" by Herman L. Hoch. The names of the Apostles are in Luke 6:13–16 and also in Acts 1:13 and 26.

Exhibit IV

Migration of the Israelites

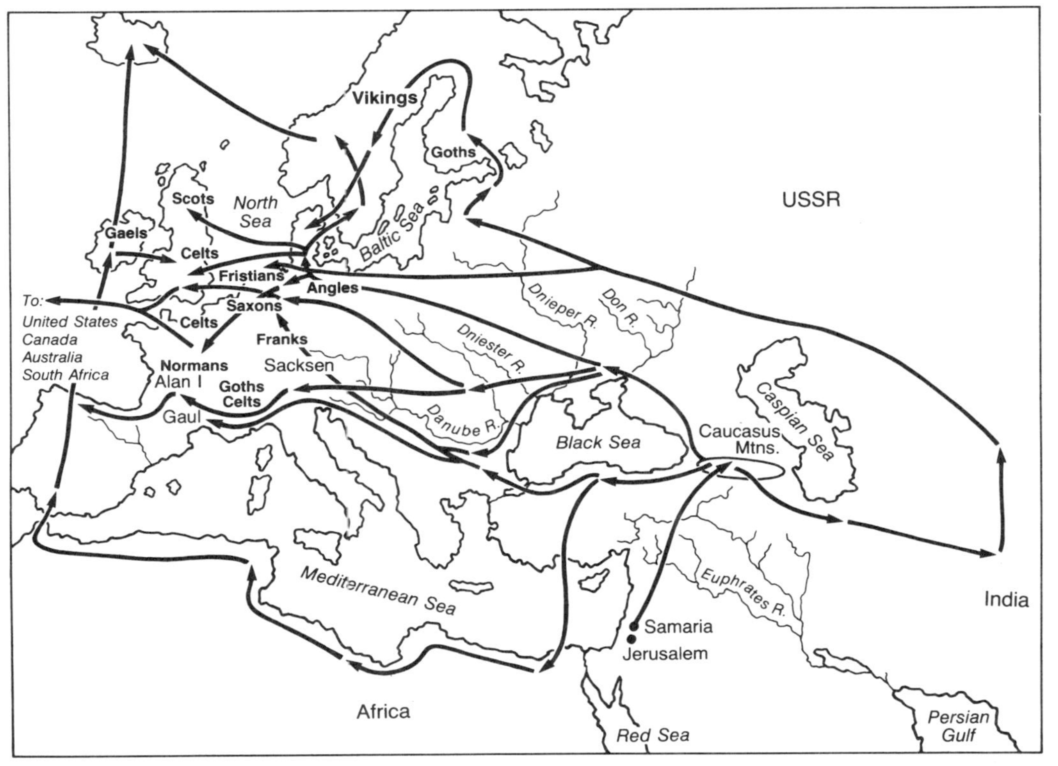

Exhibit V

Descendants of Judah to David (I Chronicles 2; Ruth 4:18–22)

Judah
Er
Onan
Shelak

Pharez—Hezron—Jerahmeel—Ram—Amminadab—Nahshon—Salma* (Salmon)—Boaz—Obed—Jesse—David* and several others to Zedekiah—Chelubai

Also sons and daughters of Jesse—Eliab—Abinadab—Shimma—Nethaneel—Raddi—Ozem—Zeruiah (Daughter)—Abigail (Daughter)

Also sons of Zeruiah—Abishai—Joab—Asahel

Zerah (Zarah)—Zimri—Ethan—Heman—Calcol—Dara
Also son of Ethan—Azariah
Also many others to King Herremon (a ruling dynasty in Ireland, then later in Scotland, then later in England)

---

*Tea-Tephi, a surviving daughter of King Zedekiah, married a son of King Herremon, traveled to Ireland, and thus David's throne continues on to this day in England after a temporary move to Scotland from Ireland and then permanently to England. When Jesus returns a second time this throne will move to Jerusalem.